Stocks
and
Shares
Simplified

A GUIDE FOR THE SMALLER INVESTOR

Stocks and Shares Simplified

A GUIDE FOR THE SMALLER INVESTOR

BRIAN J. MILLARD

London · Philadelphia · Rheine

Heyden & Son Ltd, Spectrum House, Hillview Gardens, London NW4 2JQ, UK
Heyden & Son Inc., 247 South 41st Street, Philadelphia, PA 19104, USA
Heyden & Son GmbH, Devesburgstrasse 6, 4440 Rheine, West Germany

British Library Cataloguing in Publication Data

Millard, B J
    Stocks and shares simplified.
    1. Stocks
    2. Securities
    I. Title
    332.63'22   HG4521   80-41857

    ISBN 0-85501-083-5

Typeset by Colset, Singapore, and printed in Singapore by Graphic Consultants International

Contents

Preface

The person who has yet to make an investment in the stock market, but has had a vague thought that it might be worth trying, probably holds the following ideas about the market: first, that it requires a great deal of money, at least in the thousands of pounds; second, that there is a great deal of risk involved in buying and selling shares; and third, that it requires a vast amount of time reading the City pages of his newspaper in order to understand the workings of the market and so make a profit. Many investors already engaged in buying and selling shares, albeit infrequently, if they are not dependent on the advice of others, tend to make decisions in a rather haphazard way. They may act on impulse, or because of a tip in a newspaper, or because of an overheard snippet of conversation. Such an investor is just as likely to make a loss as a profit, and the market, for him, is indeed the place of high risk that the potential investor feels it to be.

The purpose of this book is to show potential investors that they require neither vast amounts of money nor of time, and to show both them and the person already carrying out transactions that a logical approach to investment can substantially reduce the risks involved. Risk in the stock market is almost always due to bad timing of a buying or selling decision, and so the book concentrates on this aspect, helping to minimize the chances of buying at the top of the market and selling at the bottom. Of course, having decided that the time is right to buy, there is still the question of making a choice from the many thousands of shares quoted. A way is shown, which has proved successful in the past, of picking just a handful of shares from these many thousands. The book then moves on to ways in which any shares carefully bought can be sold before, as is often the case, all the profit trickles away again.

The fact that we are in the age of the microcomputer has not been forgotten, and in the Appendix there are some program listings which will reduce even further the time necessary to keep track of one's investments.

Finally, I would like to thank my wife and Mrs Valerie Jeffers for their help in the preparation of this book, and Mr Brian Marber, of Simon & Coates, for reading the early drafts and offering many helpful suggestions.

October 1980

Brian J. Millard
Berkhamsted

Chapter 1

Introduction

Investing in the stock market can be likened to joining in a game, the game being between two sides, the buyers and the sellers. Unlike other games, the *numbers* of players on each side are constantly changing. We have the option of joining one side or the other, and of changing sides at any time if we judge our side to be losing — we may be a buyer today and a seller tomorrow. This battle has been going on for hundreds of years and will continue to do as long as there is a stock market. There is no outright winning and losing side; one side may gain a temporary advantage only to see this whittled away. However, because of the choice available to him at all times, there can be an individual winner or loser in this game. The winner will see a steady gain in the value of his capital, while the loser will see his money trickle away.

The investor who has yet to make up his mind as to which side to join is like a spectator at this game. The uninformed investor will naturally assume that the side with the most players is going to win, and so when investors are clamouring to buy shares he will join their ranks. The informed investor, on the other hand, may well spot that some of the players are looking a little jaded and that the other side could well come out on top. If he has shares to sell, he would then sell while everybody else is buying everything in sight. If he has no shares to sell he will simply wait patiently as the sellers gradually come out on top, until once more he can read the signs that the buying side is about to come into its own and then join them.

The whole philosophy about stock market investment is to be ahead of the majority in your thinking and not to join the crowd when the game is poised to swing the other way. Therein lies the key to consistent profits, year after year.

Besides thinking he can see which way the game is going, what makes a person a buyer or a seller? The answer essentially can be boiled down to two emotions, greed and fear. Fear of further loss drives someone to sell their holdings, while greed, the desire to make a large profit, sends people to the market as buyers. So, in a sense, the battle in the stock market is a fight between greed and fear. As with other emotions, these two can be destructive in the sense that they blind one to the obvious and also that they are contagious. It is difficult to reason with a crowd motivated by fear or greed and the herd instinct is strong. It takes courage not to join the lemmings but this courage must not be of the blind sort — it must be based on an understanding of the facts. After all, the crowd is occasionally right!

The key to successful investing is an ability to stand apart from fear and greed and other emotions and to base one's investment posture on a reading of the signals which the market is giving. This is easier said than done. When a share which you have bought has risen in value by, say, some 50%, then there is a psychological barrier to selling, since one expects the share to go on rising. A failure to take a firm objective view of the situation can result in riding the share down to zero profit again, and perhaps even in turning the profit into a loss. There is an old adage, 'Cut your losses and let your profits run'. Many investors, through the temptation to 'wait a little longer' in the hope that their buying decision will be proved to be correct, let their losses run. It is true to say that correct selling is the most difficult aspect of stock market investment. A failure to sell at the right time can be due to various psychological difficulties — greed, a desire to be proved right, the need to avoid admitting failure etc. Of course, there are many occasions when it is wrong to sell and, by selling, a large potential profit is missed. In this case the problem is often one of worry about the degree of commitment to the particular security.

Risk is an integral part of investment and there is no doubt that the stock market is a place of greater risk than a bank deposit account or building society account. Risk can be said to be dependent mainly upon two major factors. The first of these is the quality of the equity chosen for investment, which is tied up with its volatility or historical price fluctuation. Classical investment theory equates the degree of risk with the volatility of a share. The greater the volatility, the greater the risk in investing in that share. However, this statement ignores the second important factor in investment on the stock market, which is timing. There is no doubt that a volatile share, chosen at a random point in time, has a potential for greater loss than a relatively non-volatile share. Of course, it also has a potential for a larger gain. The whole point is that in the absence of timing, investment in a very volatile share is a large gamble. Of course, under such random conditions investment in a less volatile share is also a gamble, albeit a lesser one. Note, however, that whatever the share, a gamble is still involved if no notice is taken whatsoever of correct timing, both from the point of view of general market conditions and in terms of the history of a particular share. So the most important factor in decreasing risk is in buying at the correct time. Proper timing minimizes the risk not only for non-volatile shares but for volatile ones as well. Since risk is minimized, it will make sense to invest in volatile shares since these hold out the prospect of larger gains.

In this book we are going to develop a method of correct timing of buying operations by attempting to locate major low points in the market as a whole. From such low points the majority of equities increase in value and so low risk is associated with such low points in the market.

Once a security has been bought at a time of low risk, that, of course, is not the end of the matter. Eventually there comes a time when the risk inherent in continued holding of the security becomes unacceptable and safety dictates that it be sold. In this case, not only the general state of the market becomes important but also the behaviour of the security itself. Sometimes a particular share will top out with the rest of the market and sometimes it reaches a high before or after the market as a whole. After all, it is more correct to describe the market as a market of stocks rather than a stock market. Correct timing of a sale therefore depends upon the behaviour of the particular equity and ways will be discussed of timing such sales.

Correct timing of investment buying and selling is only half of the investment story, the other half being a decision as to which securities should be bought. As already mentioned, volatility is a desirable feature since, if handled correctly, greater profits will ensue. But the problem is that not all shares which were volatile last year will necessarily be performing well this year when the market takes off from a low point; in fact, they may well be volatile in a downward sense! A criterion used in this book is to choose from a long list of the most volatile shares, those which did not retreat as much during the last few months of the decline in the market to the low point which we are establishing by our timing techniques. These can be considered to be relatively 'strong' shares and might be expected to lead the advance in the market, at least initially.

As in any other discipline, theories which are being put forward must stand up to the test of being put into practice. The techniques put forward in this book have in the past led to consistently higher profits than either random timings of random share selections, or even of correct timing in 'blue chip' companies (considered by the market to be first class investments) such as the constituents of the Financial Times 30 Index. Since history teaches us that the past gives us some guide to the future, then as far as stock market investment is concerned, a system which has worked well in the past may be expected to do the same in the future. It is not guaranteed to work, since nothing about the stock market is predictable with 100% certainty, but it will be stacking the odds in our favour. Success is virtually assured if we are right more times than we are wrong; and if we restrict our losses when we are wrong, but do not restrict our gains when we are right.

Chapter 2

Popular Forms of Investment

The stock market as a place for making money has to be judged against other forms of investment, taking into consideration several factors which are of prime importance whichever form of investment is followed. The various factors will have differing degrees of importance depending upon the personality and requirements of the particular investor. One factor is the *return* on the investment, i.e. the income obtained plus any capital appreciation during the period of investment. A second factor is the *risk* involved in making that investment, i.e. the degree of certainty that one can eventually withdraw one's money intact, together with any return on the investment. A third factor is the *degree of liquidity*, i.e. the ability to withdraw one's money at short notice if unforeseen circumstances demand it. A fourth factor is the amount of *time* necessary to gain the necessary knowledge to make a wise investment and keep a vigilant eye on its progress. A fifth factor is one's *tax position*, since the interest on some investments has already had tax deducted which is non-returnable — such a situation is better for a person in a high tax bracket than one paying little or no income tax. It should also be noted that the tax on interest earned through an investment is much higher than the tax on capital gains, the first £1000 of which is tax free at the moment.

Obviously, the ideal investment would have a high return, high liquidity, low risk and attract the minimum tax, as well as taking minimal time to manage. Life being what it is, of course, it is not possible to obtain all of these things in one investment situation and a degree of trade off of one factor against another has to be accepted, as also has a degree of diversification into several forms of investment.

The distinction between *investment* and *savings* is rather blurred. The term *savings* usually implies the frequent deposit of small sums of money. Investment simply means the employing of money to make a profit, so that savings are one form of investment. The most popular forms of investment at the moment are the following:

4

Building Society Deposits. At the time of writing the interest paid is 8% per annum, with 33% tax already deducted and not reclaimable. This interest rate is therefore equivalent to 11.94% per annum for basic tax-payers. Withdrawal is on demand or with a few days' notice. This form of investment is suitable for regular savings or the deposit of larger sums of money.

Clearing Bank Deposits. The interest rate of the big four clearing banks is about 10% per annum, and tax is not deducted at source. Seven days' notice of withdrawal is normally required. This medium is also suitable for regular small deposits.

Save-As-You-Earn (SAYE). This scheme, operated by the Building Societies, requires regular monthly savings (a fixed amount between £1 and £20). For a 5-year contract the yield at the moment is 8.3%, tax already deducted. If the money is left on deposit for a further 2 years, at the end of the 5-year period, a bonus lifts the return to 8.66% per annum.

National Savings Certificates. For the 14th issue, the annual rate is 7.59% over 4 years, tax free.

British Savings Bonds. The rate of interest is 9.5% per annum, without deduction of tax. If the bond is held for 5 years, a bonus makes the effective rate equal to 10.52% per annum. One month's notice of withdrawal is required.

Local Authority Bonds. Depending upon the local authority involved, interest rates at the time of writing run from 11.75 to 12.5% per annum. Minimum deposits vary from £250 to £5000 and the fixed term of deposit varies from 2 to 5 years.

The returns from the above investment vehicles are constantly changing but the latest rates are published, for example, in the financial sections of the quality Sunday newspapers.

In all of the above forms of investment, £1 invested is always worth £1 and the risk that the pound cannot be withdrawn on demand, or with the proper notice, is minute. Indeed, one can take the view that one's investment would only be affected by a catastrophe of such proportions that the value of money itself would be called into question. Except for local authority bonds, liquidity is high even though in some cases, for example the SAYE scheme, there may be a substantial interest penalty for early withdrawal. Demands on the investor's time are virtually zero and no specialized knowledge is necessary. Any change in interest rates is always recorded in the Press and the financial pages of the quality Sunday newspapers provide a comparison of the relative returns amongst these forms of investment.

The major disadvantage of all the above forms of investment is that during the last 5 years or so, in a period of high inflation, the yield to the standard tax-payer has not been sufficient to keep up with inflation. Two main options are open to an investor who wishes to achieve a capital growth sufficient to out-weigh the ravages of inflation: either to invest in collector's items, or to enter the stock market. However, unlike the previous types of investment, we are considering situations in which £1 invested may result in the return of £5 or 20p. In other words, there is a degree of risk involved which was not applicable to the foregoing forms of investment.

COLLECTOR'S ITEMS

Collectors are willing to pay money for an astonishing variety of items, such as antiques, banknotes, coins, early radios, old cars, paintings, porcelain, postage stamps, railway bric-à-brac, sculptures etc. To be successful with this form of investment a great deal of knowledge is necessary — knowledge which can only be gained by time and effort. The best advice is to become familiar with some small area and purchase items which are in first-class condition, are in short supply and for which there is likely to be a demand in the not too distant future. As an example of what can be achieved, and in this case without too much effort, original gramophone records of rock and roll stars of the 1950s, which sold for between 25 and 50p at the time, now change hands for anything up to £100.

Besides the need to become well informed about the chosen sector of the market, there are two other obvious disadvantages to this method of invest-ment. Firstly, with a few exceptions, a fairly long time-scale is involved if considerable gains are to be made — periods of 5 years and upwards. Secondly, it may be difficult to liquidate one's investment rapidly if the chosen area of investment is highly specialized. In coin and stamp collecting, this is not a particular problem but it should be noted that the values quoted in catalogues from the specialist firms are always on the optimistic side and are rarely realized in practice.

THE STOCK MARKET

A stock exchange deals in securities, which are of two types. On the London Stock Exchange about one-third of the securities are fixed interest stocks, issued mainly by the Government (these are called 'gilt-edged') but also by some companies (these are called debentures, loans and preference shares). The other two-thirds are the shares — called equities or ordinary shares — issued by companies. Stocks and shares are traded at prices which constantly vary, depending upon buying and selling pressure upon that particular security, just as in any other market. While, as stated, stocks are fixed interest, the dividend paid on an ordinary share can and usually does vary from year to year. Some-times no dividend may be paid for several years if the particular company is going through a bad patch. Such is the variety of securities obtainable on the Stock Exchange that degrees of risk from very low to very high exist, depending on the security. They can thus satisfy the needs of the Church Commissioners or an outright gambler. Investors can buy a security with a projected long-term growth but low yield, or the security of a virtually static company which regularly pays out high dividends. It is usual to spread the risk by investing in several securities (a 'portfolio') including both growth and high-income shares, as well as some gilt-edged.

Stock exchange securities have the advantage of high liquidity and they can be bought or sold on any day that the Stock Exchange is open but payment is neither required nor received until after the end of an account period, which is usually of 2 weeks' duration. Securities can be bought either through one's bank or by using a broker.

UNIT TRUSTS

A simple way for the small investor to enter the stock market is by buying units in a unit trust. Unit trusts have a spread of investments which is divided into equal units. The buying and selling prices, usually called 'bid' and 'offer' prices (the latter slightly higher than the former) of the units are quoted daily in the Press and reflect the market value of the trust's investments. Units can be bought directly from the managers via advertisements in the Press, or through the bank or a stockbroker. Unit trusts differ among themselves in their aims: some go for high income, some for long-term growth, some invest in specific industries and some in a particular country. The frequent advertisements usually define the aims of the trust. The daily prices rise and fall just as do those of shares, so that a loss over the short term is possible. However, the long-term trend of the whole market has been one of rising values.

A comparison of these various forms of investment is exceedingly complex when it is realized that interest rates and dividends are constantly fluctuating. If these factors are ignored, a meaningful comparison can be made in terms of the value of the capital sum committed to the original investment versus the time which has elapsed since the investment was made. Quite obviously, the buying power of the pound has declined because of inflation over the middle part of this century. Because of this a 1900 pound is worth only 5 ½p today. If the stock market is to be considered a reasonable place for investment, it needs to protect the buying power of each pound invested by means of growth in the market value of the securities held. That it can do this over the long term is illustrated by the graph shown in Fig. 2.1. This shows the buying power of the pound, an equity price index and a gilt-edged index in the form of a Consols price index. These three things are given a value of 100 for 1920, following the end of the First World War, the starting point of the graph. The pound is now worth about an eighth of its 1920 value, while £100 invested in 2 ¼% Consols in 1920 has fared even worse, being worth £4.30. By comparison, the equity price index has risen 15-fold since 1920.

A better idea of the stock market as a hedge against inflation over the shorter term is provided by Fig. 2.2. Here we have taken the cost of living and the index of share prices to each have a value of 100 in 1941. The figure shows that there

have been some periods since then when the stock market has outstripped inflation, and other periods when it has fallen behind. Over the whole period, therefore, the market has tended to oscillate about the line representing the cost of
living. We can therefore consider that the cost of living index behaves almost
like a trend line of share prices, an aspect which is discussed later in this book.
This is tantamount to saying that the cost of living is one of the factors influen-
cing share prices, or at least has been so since 1942. Trend lines can be used,
usually successfully, but sometimes not, in a predictive sense. We can therefore, justifiably, extrapolate the cost of living index forward into time. One
thing that probably nobody will dispute is that inflation is here to stay for at
least the next 5 years, so that the cost of living line is going to keep rising in the
near future. The only point at issue is at what rate it will continue to rise. Inflation may either slow down or increase over the next few years, but probably the
best guestimate is that it will continue at about the same rate for a while. Since
we can see that the index of share prices is approaching this cost of living line, it
is not unreasonable to expect that it will cross it in the near future. If we are
wrong about our projection of the forthcoming rate of inflation, and the latter
turns out to be much higher than expected, then of course we might get a situation where the share price index does not cross the line. However, if it does do
so, then based upon past behaviour of share prices, the share price index should
stay ahead of inflation for a number of years.

We can now adjust our thinking slightly about the stock market as a hedge
against inflation, and say that over the long term the market has consistently
been a good hedge but over the past few years has been less useful, although we
now expect it to pull ahead again in the immediate future.

One other aspect should be mentioned here and that is that quite obviously,
from both Figs 2.1 and 2.2, it can be seen that the growth in the stock market
has not proceeded at a steady, uninterrupted rate, but has seen a number of
short-term fluctuations, some of these of frightening proportions. As an
example, at the end of 1974 the index nose-dived to about a third of its
mid-1972 value but then recovered strongly, and reached an all-time high in
1979. An investor who through either good luck or judgement is able to take
advantage of these short-term variations can achieve a dramatic increase in the
value of his holdings compared with an investor who just buys and holds on.
Taking an average share as an example, a person who sold his shares towards
the end of 1972 could have used the proceeds to buy about three times as many
at the end of 1974.

Since the stock market offers us the chance, if we are fortunate, of making
gains much higher than the 10% or so returns we expect from the other forms of
investment discussed here, it is interesting to see the rapid way in which capital
can be built up following a number of years of consistent good fortune. Table
2.1 shows the value of £100 investment at different rates of gain from 10% to
50% per annum, over various periods of time up to 30 years. While nobody is
suggesting that we can consistently make 50% gains, year after year for 30
years, which would put us on first name terms with our bank manager, who
would honour our cheque for over £19 million, we may well make 50% for a

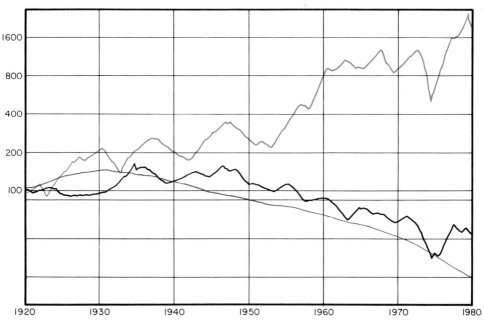

Figure 2.1. The relative performance of the pound, gilt-edged securities and equities since 1920. The black line charts the value of 2 ½ % Consols, the red line the buying power of the pound, and the green line an equity price index. Each of these starts with a base value of 100 in 1920. All values are plotted on a logarithmic ordinate. The time-scale is linear.

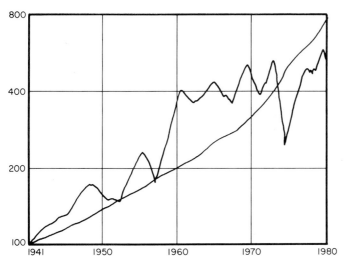

Figure 2.2. Share prices and the cost of living since 1941. The smooth line represents the cost of living while the more widely fluctuating line is the share price index. Both are given a value of 100 in 1941, and are plotted on a logarithmic scale. The time-scale is linear.

couple of years during the foreseeable future, and perhaps 20 to 30% for most of the others. If we could do this, then we would find our results moving somewhere towards the bottom right-hand corner of Table 2.1. However, we must not forget the shadow of the taxman hanging over us, and at the present time his interest starts as soon as we make over £1000 capital gains in a tax year.

Since investment in equities on the stock market is not a zero risk process, an investor should not put at risk, at least while he is learning about the market, money he cannot afford to lose. He must also not put himself in the position of having to sell securities at what may be an unfavourable time in the normal market fluctuations in order to raise cash to repair his car or for some other such emergency. A policy of investment in the stock market must go along with the maintenance of a reasonable level of savings in a highly liquid form — in a bank or building society account, for example. When this state of affairs is achieved, the only reason for selling a particular holding will be that it has reached its highest price for the time being, and is expected to fall considerably in value in the immediate future.

Table 2.1. Value of £100 invested at different rates of gain over various periods*

| Number of years | Rate of gain (or interest) | | | | |
	10%	20%	30%	40%	50%
1	110	120	130	140	150
2	121	144	169	196	225
3	133	173	220	274	338
4	146	207	286	384	506
5	161	249	371	538	759
6	177	299	483	753	1 139
7	195	358	627	1 054	1 708
8	214	430	816	1 475	2 563
9	236	516	1 060	2 066	3 844
10	259	619	1 379	2 893	5 766
20	673	3 833	19 005	83 668	332 525
30	1 745	23 738	261 999	700 036	19 175 100

*No allowance is made for taxation in this table.

Chapter 3

Is the Stock Market a Gamble?

At this point, a widely held theory about stock market investment has to be dispelled. This is that investment on the Stock Exchange is just another form of gambling. However, it is fairly easy to emphasize the distinction between gambling and informed investment. Gambling may be defined as the staking of money on situations in which the outcome is purely the workings of the laws of chance. So, for example, the chance of a 6 coming up on the throw of a die is exactly 1 in 6. Even if a six has not appeared for 50 throws, the chance for the very next throw producing a 6 has not increased, it is still 1 in 6. Now, in the case of the purchase of shares, the question is, do share prices move according to the laws of chance? Are these movements totally random? If the answer to these questions is 'yes', then we might as well bet on the football pools or horses as put our hard-earned money into shares. Fortunately for us, the answer to these questions is not 'yes', but neither is it 'no'. The best answer is that the movement of share prices is *partially* random. This is in the sense that, given a certain share price today, we cannot tell whether the price will be higher or lower tomorrow, or whether the price will be higher or lower in a year's time. What we can do, however, is say that, based upon a knowledge of the behaviour of share prices over the recent past, we can find some point in time — not necessarily today — when the price of a particular share has a very high probability of moving higher over the following few weeks or months. This is because the movement of share prices can be viewed as a random movement superimposed upon some ordered movement. A glance at any chart of a share price, or even the chart of the market as a whole in the form of the plot of the Financial Times Index, shows that share prices move in waves. The random aspect of this motion is the fact that the distance between waves, i.e. from peak to peak or trough to trough, is extremely variable, as is also the height of the waves, which may vary from a small ripple to the equivalent of a tidal wave. In addition, there is the aspect that we can have several waves superimposed upon each other, with one wave on the way down, and another, larger or smaller wave going in the opposite direction.

Part of the reason for the existence of these ripples and waves is to be found in psychology. When a share price starts to move upwards, perhaps initially due to the laws of chance that at that particular time there are slightly more buyers than sellers of that share around, then other people begin to notice and decide to buy themselves. The process gathers momentum, causing an increasing share price, until such time as some of the holders of that share start to think that it cannot go on for much longer and decide to sell. More investors become aware that the price rise is slowing down, and these in turn become sellers, so causing the share price to fall. The height of the ripples or waves will depend upon the pressure of the demand of buyers over sellers, which is random, or at least partially random. The duration of the wave is random because we do not know for how long buyers will outnumber sellers; some random political or economic event, which is totally unpredictable, may well cause the reversal of a particular trend, or there may even be no obvious reason for the change in sentiment.

The contrast between a totally random movement and the partially random movement which is the real picture for share prices can be illustrated by Fig. 3.1. In Fig. 3.1 (a) is shown the movement, over a 1-year period from the beginning of April 1978 to the end of March 1979, of the shares of Energy Services and Electronics Ltd. This is chosen as an example because it has lately been a popular share among small investors. During the period the price did not move by more than 3.5p over the course of any particular week. A computer program was set up to generate completely random price movements, of any amount from 0 to 3.5p, in 0.25p steps, either up or down. The result of this is shown in Fig. 3.1 (b).

At first glance, (a) and (b) might appear to be very similar, implying that the shares of Energy Services behave just as the random movements produced by the computer. However, a closer inspection brings out two points in which these two graphs differ. Firstly, the number of price reversals, i.e. from up to down or vice versa is much greater for the random case (28) than for the real life case, where only 16 such reversals occurred during the year. Secondly, the random price movements tend to be leading nowhere, in the sense that the price is oscillating about an (invisible) horizontal line. This would have been more obvious if we had plotted hundreds of such random points, and the reason for this journey to nowhere is because there is an equal probability of the price going up or down in a random situation. This is the same as when we spin a coin. We may get five heads and one tail in the first six spins. If we took 1000 spins, then we would get close to 500 heads and 500 tails. A gambler backing heads would be unlikely to be far ahead at the end of the session of 1000 spins. So it is with shares if they were to behave randomly: an investor would be highly unlikely to either gain or lose over a long period of time, but would come out roughly even. Now if we look at the real situation of Energy Services, we find that the price was oscillating not about a horizontal line but about an upward sloping line, not shown in the figure (such lines in the form of moving averages are shown in other examples throughout this book), but easily envisaged. An investor who bought at any time during the first half of the year could not have failed to sell at a profit in the latter half of the year. This is not to imply that all shares do this, since we could have shown some other share in which the

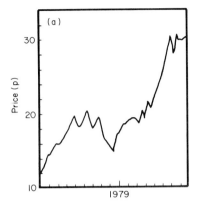
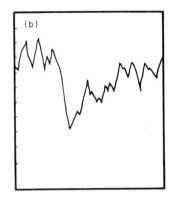

Figure 3.1. (a) The price movement of the shares of Energy Services and Electronics Ltd between April 1978 and March 1979. (b) Totally random movements of a mythical share price produced by a computer program: 52 points are plotted to simulate a year's prices.

opposite was true: an investor buying in the first half of the year could not have avoided losing if he had sold during the second half of the year. This aspect is covered more fully in Chapter 11, where it is shown how to analyse share prices for their underlying trends.

So, having agreed that share prices are partially random in their movement, and having pointed out in the last chapter that share prices on the whole are showing a long-term upward trend, we may ask ourselves if it is not sufficient to buy any share we fancy just when we feel like it, or when we have some unexpected money to spend. The answer is no, for two reasons. Firstly, it is only the market as a complete entity that is on an upward trend at the moment, and this does not mean that every share quoted on the Stock Exchange is doing the same thing. It is true that the market movement is the result of the vast majority of shares moving in that particular direction, but there is still a real chance that the very shares that you have bought are going to be the exceptions to the rule and will go down in value over a long period of time. A second point to be made is that the upward trend we are discussing is a *long-term* trend, so that if we do not envisage needing our money for 20 years or so, then we can probably get away with a policy of buying and forgetting.

The necessity for having a more logical approach to investment than just buying and selling haphazardly can be illustrated readily by reference to some actual share prices over a 4-year period. For simplicity, we can take the high and low prices for the years 1974 and 1978 of the 30 constituent companies of the Financial Times Index (see next chapter for an explanation of this Index). These values, and the average values of the share prices for each of these 2 years are given in Table 3.1. From these figures we can define three types of investor, depending upon which price he paid for the shares, and which price he received for them when he sold them.

Table 3.1. Gains or losses from buying shares in the FT 30 constituent companies in 1974 and selling in 1978

	Buy at 1974 high, sell at 1978 low			Buy at 1974 low, sell at 1978 high			Buy at 1974 middle, sell at 1978 middle		
	Buy	Sell	Gain (loss)	Buy	Sell	Gain (loss)	Buy	Sell	Gain (loss)
Allied Brew.	79	78	(1.3)	30½	93½	206.5	54.8	85.8	56.6
Beecham	273	578	111.7	104	748	619.2	188.5	663.3	251.1
Blue Circle	236	150	(36.4)	118	296	150.8	177	223	26.0
BOC	49½	63½	28.2	14½	78½	441.4	32	71	121.9
Boots	109	184	68.8	46	237	415.2	77.5	210.5	171.6
Bowater	169½	163	(3.8)	69½	213	206.5	119.5	188	34.3
BP	590	720	130.0	190	954	402.1	390	837	114.6
J. Brown	131	217	65.6	41	481	1073.2	86	349	305.8
Cadbury Schweppes	59	48	(18.6)	20	61½	207.5	39.5	54.8	38.6
Courtaulds	112½	108	(4.0)	49	130	165.3	80.8	119	47.3
Distillers	152	163	7.2	62½	215	244.0	107.3	189	76.1
Dunlop	60	63	5.0	20	90	350.0	40	76.5	91.3
EMI	135	128	(5.2)	57	190	233.3	96	159	65.6
GEC	138	235	70.3	45	344	664.4	91.5	289.5	216.4
Glaxo	420	480	14.3	184	648	252.2	302	564	86.8
Grand Metropolitan	85	87	2.4	24	121½	406.3	54.5	104.3	91.3
GKN	220	248	12.7	93	296	218.3	156.5	272	73.8
Hawker Siddeley	306	315	2.9	122	630	416.4	214	472.5	120.8
ICI	247	328	32.7	115	421	266.1	181	374.5	106.9
Imperial Group	78½	71½	(8.9)	32	89	178.1	55.3	80.3	45.1
London Brick	51	61	19.6	16	80	400.0	33.5	70.5	110.4
Lucas	115	240	108.7	41	336	719.5	78	288	269.2
M & S	227	67½	(70.3)	95	94	(1.1)	161	80.8	(49.8)
P & O	138½	76	(45.1)	56½	118½	109.7	97.5	97.3	(2.6)
Plessey	101	87	(13.9)	36	125	247.2	68.5	106	54.7
Tate & Lyle	163	164	0.6	95	218	129.5	129	191	48.1
Tube Investments	291	336	15.5	120	436	263.3	205.5	386	87.8
Turner & Newall	125	156	24.8	61	209	242.6	93	182.5	96.2
UDS	97½	82	(15.9)	41	111	170.7	69.3	96.5	39.4
Vickers	121	160	32.2	65	211	224.6	93	185.5	99.5
Average gain			17.7%			320.8%			96.5%

1. Mr Lucky. In 1974 this man decided to buy shares in each of the 30 companies. Through good luck he just happened to choose the time when each of the shares was at its low value for the year. In 1978, Mr Lucky thought it was about time that he took his profit in order to shift his investment to some other enterprise. He fortunately chose a time to sell just as share prices were at their peak. Table 3.1 shows that Mr Lucky made an overall gain of 320.8% from these 30 shares over the period.

2. Mr Unlucky. In 1974 Mr Unlucky decided to buy shares in all 30 companies of the FT Index. However, everything Mr Unlucky touches crumbles to dust. He thought that share prices, already at their high values, were headed forever upwards, and bought at the 1974 peaks. Four years later, Mr Unlucky thought that share prices, already on their way down, were going to fall even further, and so he sold out at what turned out to be the bottom prices for 1978 for the 30 shares. Table 3.1 shows that Mr Unlucky made an overall gain of 17.7% for the period.

3. Mr Average. Mr Average also decided to buy shares in 1974. He happened to decide to do this just as the shares were at their mid-points for the year. Four years later, Mr Average decided to sell out and take his profit, since the financial section of his Sunday newspaper said that the economy was beginning to look unhealthy. He got out just as the 30 shares were at their mid-points for 1978. Mr Average made a profit of 96.5% over the period.

Of these three different types of investor, one was unfortunate enough to make a gain of only 17.7% over the period and would have been better off putting his money in the building society; one was lucky enough to make a gain of 320%, i.e. increased his original investment by a factor of four; the third, average, investor nearly doubled his money in the period.

Now, of course, most of us would fall into the category of Mr Average, because for both of the years 1974 and 1978 — in the fact for any year — the share prices spend only a few days or weeks at the extreme high or low values. Most of the time they are somewhere in between, so we are more likely to buy or sell, if we do so in a random manner, somewhere at the middle of the price range for that particular year.

Another, equally important aspect in investment is the correct *selection* of shares. Again we can use Table 3.1 to illustrate our three types of investor. This time we shall assume that each investor selects five shares from the list of 30 and we can look at the resulting performances.

1. Mr Lucky. This man was lucky enough to select the very five shares which performed the best over the period. He chose Beecham (619.2% gain), BOC (441.4% gain), John Brown (1073.2% gain), GEC (664.4% gain) and Lucas (719.5% gain). So Mr Lucky's portfolio of five shares, bought at their 1974 lows and sold at their 1978 highs showed a staggering 703.5% gain over the period, so that he increased his capital by a factor of over eight.

2. Mr Unlucky. This poor man unwittingly chose the five worst performers over the period. He selected Blue Circle (loss 36.4%), Cadbury Schweppes (loss 18.6%), Marks & Spencer (loss 70.3%), P & O (loss 45.1%) and UDS (loss 15.9%). Mr Unlucky's loss over the period in buying those shares at their 1974 highs and selling at their 1978 lows was a disappointing 37.3%

3. Mr Average. Mr Average chose the shares which were in the middle of the range of performance. He bought Distillers (76.1% gain), Dunlop (91.3% gain), Glaxo (86.8% gain), Grand Metropolitan (91.3% gain) and Tube Investment (87.8% gain). He bought these at their average 1974 prices and sold at their average 1978 prices. This resulted in an overall gain of 86.7%

These results show us how important it is to make a correct choice of shares. This correct choice improved Mr Lucky's gain from 320.8% to 703.5%, effectively more than doubling his profits. On the other hand, a bad choice of shares was disastrous for Mr Unlucky, turning his small gain of 17.7% into a large loss of 37.3%. In the case of Mr Average, we would not expect the gains from five shares chosen as being in the middle of the group of 30 in terms of performance to be very much different from the behaviour of the group as a whole, since of course mathematically speaking, the average of the 30 is going to end up somewhere in the middle of their price ranges. This turns out to be the case in practice.

No doubt at this point, most of us would probably say that we would be quite happy to be in Mr Average's position, with a gain of somewhere between 86.7% and 96.5%. The point is, though, that Mr Average did not make his gains through exercising his intelligence, but merely through the good luck to do all the right things at the right time. There is no guarantee that luck would run the same way for us, and we may well turn out to be about as successful as Mr Unlucky. As serious investors, a policy based simply on luck should have no part to play in our investment philosophy. So we have to develop methods which are based upon logical timing and selection procedures which themselves are made as objective as possible.

As far as timing is concerned, there are of course two areas in which we have to exercise judgement: knowing when to buy and when to sell. It is interesting that the tipsters in most newspapers have a blind spot when it comes to selling shares which they have tipped strongly as buying situations sometime earlier. You are most unlikely, however closely you study the financial pages of your newspaper, to find a recommendation to sell a particular share, whether it is a share which that columnist implored you to buy at the beginning of the year, or another one which he did not mention as a buy, but which is known to be popular amongst small investors. A moment's thought will tell you that buying and selling are equally critical operations and correct buying procedures can be ruined by a failure to sell at the right time. It is no use telling your friends how clever you were to buy XYZ at 120p when they reached 200p if you are still left holding them when they have plunged to 90p. Certainly you were clever to have bought at 120 but you would have been cleverer still if you had sold at 190 when XYZ started to fall back from their peak.

The two areas of buying and selling require different approaches, and so in this book separate chapters are devoted to when to buy and when to sell. It is amply demonstrated that it is possible to develop methods which consistently give us a buying signal at the low end of the price range of a share and consistently give us a selling signal at the top end of the range. It is certain, therefore, that we can, by using these methods, improve upon the performance of the average investor, who just picks his buying time, selling time and the share in question, more often than not at random.

It should be stressed, and a study of the methods outlined in the two chapters on buying and selling will underline this, that it is not possible *at the time* to determine that a share is at its low or high value. The end of an upward or downward trend in a share price is a random event. We have already mentioned the *partially random* nature of share price movements, and pointed out that the existence of trends is evidence for the partially predictable nature of share prices. Once the trend has been under way for some time, it becomes more and more probable that it is going to end. It is the exact time of the ending of the trend that is unknown until after it has occurred and a new trend in the other direction, or even sideways, is in being. The best timing methods will tell us as soon as possible — in terms of days or a few weeks at most — that the direction of movement has changed. By knowing as soon as possible that the direction has changed, we will be able to buy at prices not very far upwards from the actual

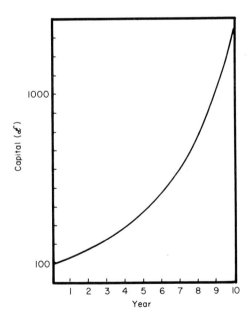

Figure 3.2. The growth in capital over a 10-year period when a consistent gain of 30% is made each year.

low and sell at prices not very far down from the high value.

The selection procedure which we put forward in this book is based upon two premises. Firstly, that shares which vary the most between their high and low values and have done for a number of years, will continue to do the same in the future, at least in the near future. A second consideration is that some shares are obviously not falling as much as the rest of the market during a general decline. These shares can be considered to be amongst the strongest in the market and therefore should advance the most when the market recovers. Once again, it is amply demonstrated that this selection procedure is a vast improvement upon a random selection just based upon personal feeling or newspaper tips.

An investor who follows the rules for selection and timing of purchases and sales outlined in the following chapters should hope to see a return on his investment considerably higher than the rate of inflation.

The rapid rise in the value of capital which occurs when compounding such a gain each year is shown in Fig. 3.2. An investor starting with £100 will be worth £1379 after 10 years, while starting with £1000 would see him £13 790

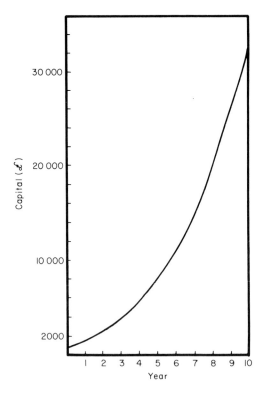

Figure 3.3. The growth in capital over a 10-year period when a consistent gain of 30% is made and additional sums are added. In this case the starting amount is £1000 and £500 is added each year.

to the good after 10 years.

Probably most investors would be tending to add an amount each year to their original investment. In this case, the capital appreciates at a tremendous rate. As an example we could take an investor who starts with £1000 and adds to this a sum of £500 each year. His holdings will follow the curve shown in Fig. 3.3 if he makes a gain of 30% each year. At the end of 10 years his £30 000+ should enable him to look life's little financial disasters in the eye! Of course, these figures assume the lucky investor is living in tax exile and it should be pointed out that the first £1000 of capital gains is tax free, and the next £4000 carries a 15% rate of tax, the next £4500 carries 50% and for gains of £9500 and above, the whole gain is taxed at a flat 30% at the present time.

Chapter 4

Buying, Selling and Reading the News

To most people the Stock Exchange is something of a mystery. It is a place where fortunes are made overnight, whose members live in large houses somewhere in Surrey and travel to the City in a first class compartment. While some of this is true, it is not generally realized how many people are directly and indirectly involved in the workings of the Stock Exchange. Some 3 – 4 million individuals own shares directly; for example, ICI has about half a million shareholders. The rest of the population are indirectly involved in security ownership through the big institutions, such as life insurance offices, pension funds, trade unions, building societies, banks etc. These have huge resources to invest, tens of millions of pounds each week for life insurance offices alone, and a large proportion of these funds are used to buy stocks and shares. There can hardly be a person in the UK who has no life insurance, does not belong to a pension fund, does not belong to a trade union, and does not deposit money in a bank or building society, however temporarily. Even if such a person exists, he is a resident of a country whose government raises money through the Stock Exchange, and the company he works for may well do the same.

How the idea of a Stock Exchange began is not known, but it was tied up with the increase in trade from Elizabethan times onwards. All sorts of enterprises grew up in which numbers of people wished to participate. Since new participants may have wished to pull out of an enterprise or even invest more money in it, a market-place grew up in which buyers and sellers could meet, usually through an agent. As governments also wished to raise loans, usually in order to wage war, this function also became part of the working of the market.

From its original beginnings as a part of the market place in the Royal Exchange the Stock market moved to its own premises in 1773, using the name 'Stock Exchange' and then to its present site at the beginning of the nineteenth century. Today, the Stock Exchange occupies a 26 storey tower block.

The workings of the Stock Exchange are peculiar to London. In New York, where Wall Street has the largest exchange in the world, the buying and selling of stocks and shares is carried out by stock brokers who deal with each other. In London, brokers have to use special dealers known as jobbers. The jobbers are stationed at pitches on the 'Floor' of the Stock Exchange, and are responsible for setting buying and selling prices. Only a few jobbers will deal with any one security. A jobber is only interested in a particular group of securities and will buy or sell these. Jobbers have to judge market trends, and their profit or loss depends on the difference between buying and selling prices, which can vary by the minute.

The broker's job is to carry out the wishes of his client, who may be a buyer or a seller of a particular security. He goes to each of the jobbers who deal in that security and ascertains the buying and selling prices quoted by each jobber. The latter, incidentally, does not know, when he quotes prices, whether the broker wishes to buy or sell that particular security. The broker then buys or sells, as necessary, the security with the jobber quoting the most attractive price. The broker will always obtain the best deal possible for his client, who may be you, the individual, or a bank acting on your instruction, or a big institutional investor. Both jobber and broker note the bargain in a little book, and the shares are then yours, if you are buying, or the proceeds are yours, if you are selling. However, as explained later, the paperwork for the transaction takes a while to catch up, but if you are a buyer, you may still sell your shares, the same day if you wish, before you receive your share certificates.

The beginner, making his first few purchases and sales of shares, can carry out these operations by walking into his bank and then giving instructions in writing to buy or sell so many shares of X. Within a day or so, he will receive a contract note setting out the transaction and the total sum to be paid (including stamp duty, commission etc.) or the total being credited to his account. These moneys will not be due until settlement day, which is normally the Tuesday 11 days after the end of the fortnightly account. Thus shares purchased on the first day of the account will not have to be paid for for about 3 weeks. Eventually the share certificates will arrive at the bank and be retained by them unless you specifically ask for them.

For the serious investor, it is best to have your own broker, since besides the simple operation of buying and selling, the broker provides a number of services. He can tell you about the standing of the individual companies, the industrial sectors which are progressing the most rapidly, current economic trends and the like. You cannot just walk into a broker's office, however, and ask him to deal for you. You can either be introduced by someone who is a client of the broker, or you can write to the Secretary of the Stock Exchange, London, EC2, and ask for a list of brokers. From this list select a broker (the Stock Exchange will not recommend one) and write to him asking if he will take you as a client, giving the name and address of your bank as a reference. Once he is happy about your ability to pay for any securities you buy, you can either telephone or write your instructions to buy or sell as necessary.

The instructions to your broker should be as clear as possible, and normally, in the event of buying, you should quote a limit above which you are not prepared to buy. Otherwise your broker may be buying the shares at the top of a daily price range, which would not have happened if you had set a limit which was lower than this. Your broker may well call you to say he cannot buy at the limit you have set, and quotes the best possible price he can obtain. You can either accept that and tell him to go ahead and buy at that price, or ask him to keep the limit on for a day or so. However, one has to be realistic, and if the market price of your shares is improving constantly, either buy at the best price your broker quotes you or look for some other share.

The cost of buying shares is somewhat higher than the cost of selling, because of government stamp duty on purchases. As a rough guide, the detailed costs of buying and selling 300 shares at a buying price of 136p and a selling price of 124p are given below:

Buying		Selling	
300 shares @ 136p,		300 shares @ 124p,	
consideration	£408.00	consideration	£372.00
add transfer stamp	9.00	less contract stamp	0.10
add contract stamp	0.10	less commission	7.00
add commission	7.00	less VAT on	
add VAT on		commission	1.05
commission	1.05		
Total	£425.15	Total	£363.85

So, taking into account the actual cost of buying the shares, you have payed about 141.7p per share as opposed to the quoted price of 136p, and receive about 121p per share compared with the quoted price of 124p. Before you can make a profit on a 'round trip' of buying and then selling the same share, the price would have to rise from 136p, the buying price, to a selling price of about 145p, i.e. a gain of about 7%. If you hold the shares for a period which includes the payment of a dividend, the latter may well offset these buying and selling costs.

At some point, preferably before you buy shares, but certainly after you own a piece of a company, you will be following the fortunes of your selected company in the financial press. You will also receive, from time to time, glossy brochures containing balance sheets etc., and so it is going to be essential for you to understand the entries in the share price pages of newspapers, and have some ability to extract the essential data from company reports.

READING THE FINANCIAL PRESS

The world of finance, as any other activity, generates its own jargon and short-hand which makes it difficult for the newcomer to understand what is being said. Appendix C is a glossary which lists just about all the expressions and words you are likely to come across. There is one area, however, which needs some expansion, and that is an explanation of the various columns of figures normally found in the share prices pages of newspapers. A few typical entries are shown in Table 4.1.

Table 4.1 Typical headings and figures on the share price pages of various newspapers

1979 High	Low	Share	Price	Change	Div.(net)	Cover	Yield (gross)	P/E
30	14½	Dubilier 5p	30	—	1.1	2.8	5.5	7.3
£90	118	EMI 50p	118	− 15	9.38	0.7	12.2	16.2
£106½	£91½	EMI 8% Conv.'81	£92	—	£4½	12.0	9.4	—
375	159	Electrocomps 10p	373	+ 1	2.55	8.5	1.0	17.1

The figures in the columns 1979 'High' and 'Low' are the highest and lowest prices achieved by the security during the year. At the end of the year, in order to achieve a carry over, the column would be headed, for example 1979/80, but the 1979 figures will be dropped usually round about mid-April, at the end of the stock exchange account in which the last day of the income tax year falls. These figures are useful in telling us where today's price stands in relation to the highs and lows, i.e. is the share making a new high, or a new low, or has it risen some way from its low value?

Under the heading 'Share' we find the name of the company and the type and nominal value of the share. In this book we are only concerned with ordinary shares, which simply have a name such as Dubilier 5p, which means the shares had a nominal value of 5p when first issued. The nominal value, if not given is taken to be 25p. For EMI,* however, we can see there are two entries, EMI 50p and EMI 8% Conv.'81 — short for 8% Convertible 1981. The EMI 50p are, of course, ordinary shares of nominal value 50p, but the other entry is for a loan stock. When this was issued, the nominal or par value of the stock was £100, although it might have been issued at a price slightly more or less than this. The interest rate was fixed at 8% per £100 of stock, so that the present holder gets £8 per annum for each £100 of stock irrespective of the price he may have had to pay for it, which varied between £91 ½ and £106 ½ in 1979. The 'Convertible 1981' label means that the holder has the option to convert the stock into ordinary shares, and that the maturity date is 1981.

The terms for conversion for the loan stocks of companies will differ from company to company. Loan stocks are more secure than ordinary shares in the sense that the interest will be paid, whereas dividends on ordinary shares may not, and the loan stock will be repaid first before ordinary shares, but after loan stocks in terms of repayment when a company runs into difficulties are

* EMI have now been taken over, and do not have a separate quote.

so-called 'Preference' shares. Not many of these have voting rights in the company.

It follows from the above that ordinary shares are the risk capital, so that holders do well in terms of dividends if the company is prospering, but do badly when things go wrong. Most companies do not pay out all their surplus profits in the form of dividends, but hold on to part of them. Sometimes these accumulated surpluses are issued as 'free' shares, usually called 'scrip issue' or a 'capitalization issue'. Most ordinary shares carry voting rights in the company, but those few that do not are usually called 'A' shares in the entry under 'Shares', for example Burtons the Tailors have a voting share, Burton 50p and a non-voting share, Burton 'A' nv 50p.

The column headed 'Price' gives the closing price of that share the previous day. It usually represents a middle value between the buying and selling price, so that if you are buying, you will almost certainly have paid a little more, and if you are selling, will receive a little less than the listed price. The 'change' column is simply whether the price has moved up (+) or down (−), and the amount of the movement since the previous day's close. An unchanged price may have a hyphen, row of dots or be left blank.

The 'Dividend net' is the dividend actually paid per share. Usually dividends are paid twice yearly, the first payment being called the interim and the second payment the final dividend. The cover is the ratio of the profit the company made to the amount of money it paid out in dividends, so telling us how much of the company profits found their way to the shareholders.

The gross yield is derived from the dividend relative to the share price before applying advanced Corporation Tax at the rate pertaining at the time.

The P/E (price to earning) ratio is calculated by dividing the earnings per share into the share price. Thus supposing a company made £20.5 million, and its ordinary capital is £80 million, the shares having a par value of 25p. If the present share price is say 90p, then the P/E ratio is:

$$\frac{0.90 \times 80}{20.5 \times 0.25} = 14.0$$

SHOULD WE PAY MUCH ATTENTION TO FINANCIAL NEWS?

So far we have been dealing with facts as reported in the financial press, i.e. dividends and share prices. However, the other aspect of the financial press, the airing of opinions and reasons for the behaviour of the market, has to be taken very cautiously. This can be illustrated very easily by quoting the reasons for a movement of the Financial Times Index, one barometer of the market, over a fairly short period of time, as given in the same newspaper.

1. Fears of an impending general election sent investors diving for cover. The Index fell 6.7, on sustained selling.
2. Confidence in the near certainty of a general election with a consequent Conservative victory caused what some brokers described as panic buying in

markets yesterday. The Index recorded a gain of 10.2.

3. The large rise in the value of the pound on foreign exchange markets has led to increasing nervousness about the ability of British Industry to remain competitive in overseas markets. The gloom was reflected in stock markets by a fall of 8.2 in the FT Index.

4. The increasing value of the pound saw foreign investors piling into gilts yesterday. The confidence spilled over into the equity markets, which saw its largest 1-day rise, 8.5, for several months.

5. The prospect of a give-away budget fuelling a mini consumer boom had investors out in force yesterday. The stores sector registered some solid gains and the index rose six points.

6. Uncertainty about the content of the forthcoming budget resulted in a downward drift in the markets yesterday. The stores sector was particularly hard-hit, with Marks & Spencer shedding 5p. The Index ended the day 4.7 points down.

7. John Bull & Co. announced profits up 30% on last year. The final dividend was increased 50% to 4.5p to give a total of 8.5p. The shares fell 3p to 115.

8. The Chairman's statement underlined the fact that 1980 will be a difficult trading year. The value of the pound causing difficulty in foreign markets allied to the deepening world recession makes it likely that a number of plants will have to go on short time. The shares gained 2p to 258p.

The above statements fall into two categories. In the first six, the commentators are trying to square the behaviour of the market as a whole with the overall political or economic climate. It makes no sense that one day a strong pound can be considered to be a reason for selling shares, while a few days later a strong pound is a reason for buying shares. The reasons for the behaviour of the market are almost certainly more subtle than that.

In the next two statements, the shares appear to behave in a contrary fashion to that which one would expect from the company news. The reason is that the news has already been either known for certain by those with the right contacts, or has been guessed at by the 'clever money'. Thus the good news or bad news has already been discounted in the share price.

The essential point which the foregoing is meant to convey is that an investor who buys or sells according to financial news is unlikely to be successful. An investor has to join the ranks of those people who are ahead of the news. How? Well, quite straightforwardly, in fact, if one makes the reasonable assumption that the activities of those investors who are ahead of the market will be reflected by a movement in the price of the shares concerned. It is by following the prices of shares that we can therefore make buying or selling decisions in good enough time to make a superior profit compared with those who wait until it is too late. The breaking of good or bad news is then more or less irrelevant to us, since we will have already taken action. In a great many cases we will not be surprised by such news, since we will be very well aware of the price movements caused by those who either have inside knowledge or have made educated guesses.

Chapter 5

When to Buy

The market in securities, as any other market, is a place of shifting values, depending upon supply and demand, which in turn reflect investor psychology. In order to come to any conclusion about the market we have to have some means of measuring it. The most widely quoted measurement of the market is the Financial Times Industrial Ordinary (FT 30) Index. The Index is derived from the prices of 30 leading equities, covering all sectors of the market. These are listed in Table 5.1.

Table 5.1. Constituents of the Financial Times Index

Allied Breweries	Distillers	London Brick
Beecham Group	Dunlop	Lucas
Blue Circle	EMI	Marks & Spencer
BOC International	GEC	P & O
Boots	Glaxo	Plessey
Bowater	Grand Metropolitan	Tate & Lyle
BP	GKN	Tube Investments
John Brown	Hawker Siddeley	Turner & Newall
Cadbury Schweppes	ICI	UDS Group
Courtaulds	Imperial Group	Vickers

Since the market is composed of thousands of shares, it may be asked whether the FT Index truly reflects the state of the market. In order to decide on this it is necessary to look at how the Index is calculated from the prices of its 30 constituents. The FT 30 Index is a geometric mean of the prices of its components. Because of this, it has a built-in pull downwards, i.e. it tends to be rather pessimistic of market behaviour. This can be illustrated by imagining a similar index constructed from only two shares. Suppose the shares are both valued at 200p. The index is then $\sqrt{(200 \times 200)} = 200$.

Now, if one share moves up to 300p and the other down to 100p, then an investor holding both of these would see no change in his total investment, since their average price would still be 200p. The new index, however, would be $\sqrt{(300 \times 100)}$ = 173.2. Thus the index has fallen although the value of the portfolio has remained unchanged. You can work out for yourself, that, except if the two prices move exactly the same amount, this index is always less than the usual arithmetic average, calculated by taking half of the sum of the two prices.

There are several other indices available, for example the FT Actuaries All Share Index. Like the FT 30 Index, none of these tells the real truth. The FT 30 Index has the advantage that it is widely quoted, appearing in all those newspapers that have a City section, is given in the financial news on radio and television and is available via the telephone recorded service. Because of its ready availability, we shall use it in this book as a means of deciding on market turning points, but always bearing in mind that it is somewhat pessimistic.

THE PAST: A HELP WITH THE FUTURE

The only evidence upon which we can base any prediction of the immediate or long-term future of the market is by a study of its past history. The past gives us an indication of how the market reacted to various factors and it is not too far-fetched to believe that a recurrence of the same factors will have an effect on the market. Of course, from time to time new factors occur which have not been encountered before, such as the impact of North Sea oil but these can be treated on their merits. We are concerned with the trends that develop as a result of these various factors, and especially with the fact that the trends last for appreciable time periods, so that when their existence is determined, there is still plenty of movement left in the same direction. Because of this, it is then possible to take an investment position with a high degree of certainty of profit.

An important feature of the market is its volatility, which we may define as the rate at which it goes up or down. We can gain an impression of this from plotting the Financial Times Index over a period of time. If the Index rises or falls a substantial amount, say 20% or so, in a period of a few days, then obviously we would describe it as very volatile, whereas if it took 5 years to rise or fall this amount, then we would say it was involatile. From our point of view, the degree of volatility is crucial to the determination of the time for which we remain invested, i.e. are we going to buy one week and sell the next, or are we talking in terms of periods of years between these two actions? This question of volatility is also important in deciding for how long we have to follow the market before we can decide if it is rising or falling. To illustrate this point, the daily plot of the Index for one week (2 – 7 October 1978) is shown in Fig. 5.1. Now, is it possible to decide from this whether the market is rising or falling? Well, the market does appear to be going up by virtue of the fact that it started the week at 500.6 and ended up at 503.0. Now, remembering that we have to have a gain of at least 5% in order to clear our buying and selling commissions, then, if we look at the Index as a share in which we can invest, clearly we would

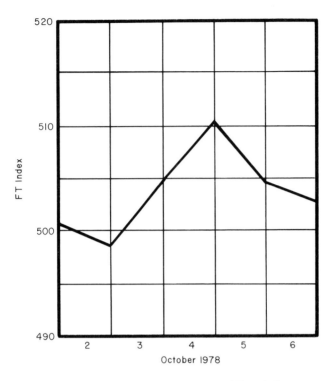

Figure 5.1. The daily closing value of the Financial Times Index over a period of 5 days in October 1978.

not have made a profit in buying on Monday and selling on Friday, or even selling on the Wednesday when the index reached 511 or so. Figure 5.1 is fairly typical of the market, in the sense that it is extremely rare, say on no more than 3 or 4 weeks a year, for the market to rise or fall by 5% or more in a week. There are, of course, many individual shares that do much better or much worse than that, but at the moment we are only concerned with the whole market. So, Fig. 5.1 tells us one thing — our buying and selling must cover a larger period than a week if we are to make a profit, since, with only a few exceptions which it would be difficult to predict in advance, the market is not volatile enough to deal on such a short time-scale. Now, can we use Fig. 5.1 to tell us something else, namely if we are contemplating buying, is that particular week a good week to buy, since we have shown a week in which the Index has risen over the 5-day period? Conversely, if we had shown a figure in which the Index had fallen to about the same extent over the week, would that have told us if it was the time to sell if we had been holding some shares? The answer is that next week's market may or may not continue in the same direction. For the week we have been discussing, where the market appeared to be rising, it transpired that that was the highest point reached for the next 6 months. The market fell from that point to a low of around 450 by February 1979 and did not come back up to the 500 level until March 1979. Quite obviously then, the behaviour of the market over 1 week tells us virtually nothing about the climate for investment. One may well ask at this point if we can ever decide which way the market is moving. The answer is yes, but only if we look at a large enough time period, the time period being sufficient to encompass much greater movements in the market. From past history, there frequently occur periods in which swings of 20% in the FT Index occur within some 3 months or so. Thus, in order to decide on the current direction of the market, we should look at the last 3 months' weekly closing values of the Index at the very least and preferably even a longer period.

For our purposes, since we are trying to establish as good a picture of the market as possible, we should look at a time-scale of the order of 10 years or so. Already in Chapter 2 we have shown how shares have performed compared with gilt-edged securities and the cost of living since the period since 1919 (Fig. 2.1). The disadvantage of Fig. 2.1 is that although it gives an indication that the market has zig-zagged up and down, and that the underlying trend is upwards, it does not show us the fine detail of the week-to-week variations. In order to do this, the movement of the FT Index since 1967 is shown in Fig. 5.2. The immediate impact of this figure is that the market has moved in waves, with troughs every 4 years or longer apart. Superimposed upon these large waves we have smaller ones, of a few months or so duration, and finally upon these we have ripples which are normally of a few weeks' duration. The large waves, small waves and ripples may not always be moving in the same direction — we may have small wave which is falling, taking prices down, but is superimposed on a large wave which is trending upwards. In such a case, our shares may show a

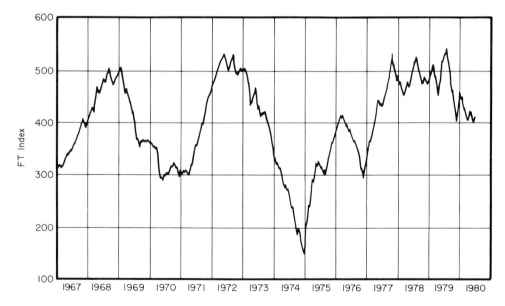

Figure 5.2. The movements of the Financial Times Index over the period since 1967. The vertical scale is linear.

loss in the short term, but the price will eventually recover. On the other hand, the small wave may be causing an upward lift to prices when the underlying trend is downwards. To buy at such a time with a view to holding for a reasonable length of time may see the initial profit quickly eroded. Quite obviously, timing of our investment buying is absolutely crucial and in this chapter we are going to develop methods which will enable us to take advantage of large waves, small waves and even the ripples of a few weeks' duration. We will see that it is possible to use a ripple profitably even when the underlying longer-term trend of the market is downwards.

These waves and ripples are the result of a struggle between two groups of people. In stock market parlance they are called 'bulls' and 'bears'. Bulls are optimists, who think that at this particular moment, share values are set for an increase and so they buy. Bears think the opposite, that the market is about to go down and that the time has come to sell. Sometimes they feel so strongly about this that they sell shares they have not got, with a view to buying them back later at a lower price to pass back to the previous buyer via the broker. At any one time, there will always be these two sorts of operators in the stock market, but they will rarely be in balance. When bulls predominate, the market will go up and when bears predominate, the market will go down. The ratio of these two sets of people will vary according to their interpretation of various news items, both political and business, upon other investors, as well as their overall feeling about the economy in general and the stock market is particular.

If, for the moment we ignore the short-term variations, an idealized version of the FT Index over a number of years would look like that in Fig. 5.3. From

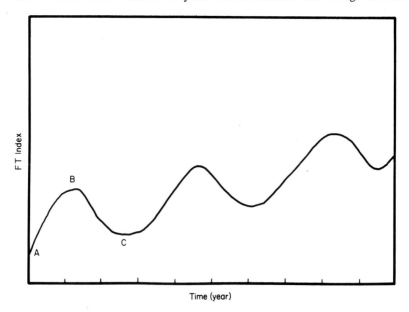

Time (year)

Figure 5.3. An idealized version of the movements of the Financial Times Index over a period of years.

point A to B, a bull phase, more and more investors and investing institutions become filled with optimism about share prices, and put more and more money into the market, pushing up share prices and hence the Index. At point B, the smart operators, and those of you who have taken note of the contents of this book, will realize that it cannot go on for ever and that it is time to get out. Gradually the amount of selling starts to outweigh the amount of buying and the market and Index starts on a downward journey. The degree of pessimism then also starts to increase. Many investors get burnt by failing to sell at, or soon after, point B, and watch their share values fall to point C. At this point, many of them are so shattered by the experience that they sell out, and never invest in the market again. By the time point C is reached, many of the experienced investors realize that the fall has to end some time and they piece together enough optimistic facts from the business news to convince themselves that it is time to start buying again. This starts a new upward trend, which develops its own momentum as more and more investors climb on the bandwagon to begin the heady climb again. The whole process repeats itself time and time again over the years, while some investors get richer, and some poorer.

These variations are nothing to be frightened about and are the very thing from which much larger profits can be made, rather than a situation in which the market is climbing slowly in a fairly straight line. This can be illustrated by putting some theoretical (but fairly typical) values to the Index, and pretending that the Index is a share in which we are investing. We can then compare the results obtained by an investor who buys at the beginning of the long term and sells at the end with those obtained by someone who buys and sells several times at the appropriate intermediate bottoms and tops.

Point	Corresponding FT Index
A	200
B	300
C	250
D	350
E	300
F	400
G	350

If we invest £200 at point A, we can then sell at point B for £300. At point C this £300 will then buy 300/2.50 = 120 shares. The 120 shares will rise in value and be worth 120 × £3.50 = £420 at point D. This £420 will buy 420/3.00 = 140 shares at point E. These 140 shares at point F are worth 140 × £4.00 = £560.

Therefore, starting with £200 at point A, by a series of buying and selling at the troughs and peaks, the investment becomes worth £560, i.e. a gain of 180%. Compared with this, an investor who buys at point A, investing £200 will be able to realize £400 at point F, i.e. he has a profit of 100%.

What may be a surprise to some investors is that a profit can still be made by buying and selling at the appropriate times even when the longer term trend is downwards. Take the following values of the FT Index at points A to F as an example:

Point	Corresponding FT Index
A	350
B	400
C	300
D	350
E	250
F	300

Suppose in this case, to make the figures simpler, that we invest £350 at point A. The shares can be sold at point B for £400. This will buy 133 shares at point C, which rise in value to 133 × £3.50 = £465.5 at point D. This amount of money will buy 186 shares at point E where they are 250 each, and finally they can be sold for £558.6 at F. Therefore the initial investment has made a gain of 59.6%. Compared with this, an investor who bought at A and sold at F would have made a loss of 42.9%.

So, in both of these cases, the members of the buy and hold brigade would have come out way behind an investor who takes advantage of the intermediate ups and downs in share values. Of course, in these calculations, the cost of buying and selling shares has been neglected, but it is fair to take the view that the dividends yielded by an average portfolio more or less cover the costs of the various transactions, so that these costs can be considered to have a minimal effect on the profit and loss picture.

The situation we were discussing is rather an artificial one, mainly for two reasons. Firstly, it is never possible to buy consistently at an exact bottom and sell at an exact top, and anyone who claims to be able to do this can probably also walk on water. Secondly, we have been discussing not an actual share, but the market in general. The market in general is of course composed of thousands of shares, and while the market as a whole is rising, most, but not all of these shares will do the same, although some will gain more than others. Conversely, when the market is falling, most shares will fall, although a few will manage to register gains during that time.

This can be illustrated by Fig. 5.4, in which is shown the plots of several hypothetical shares, and the plot of the overall market in these shares, as indicated by an average of the prices of all these shares. In what we might call the topping region, which is a few weeks or even months either side of the actual top of the average of all these shares, we have shown one share topping out in advance of the market, one share topping out at the same time as the market, one share topping out later than the market, and finally a 'rogue' share which is going its own way. Next there is a bottoming region, which again is a few weeks or months either side of the market bottom. Once more, we have a share that bottoms in advance of the market, one share bottoming at the same time, one share reaching its lowest point later than the market, and in addition, our rogue share has been steadily rising while the rest of the market has been falling. It

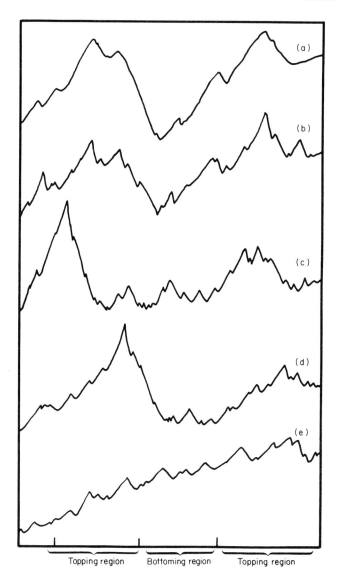

(a)

(b)

(c)

(d)

(e)

Topping region   Bottoming region   Topping region

Figure 5.4. The share price movements of some hypothetical shares over a period of time: (a) an average for the market as a whole, (b) the movement of a fairly typical share; (c) an early topping share; (d) a late topping share; and (e) a 'rogue' share behaving contrariwise to the market.

should be pointed out here that a share which tops out ahead of the market does not necessarily bottom ahead of the market, and the same is true of a share which tops out later than the market. As far as we are concerned, whether a share tops out early or late after we have bought it is irrelevant, for each share will be giving its signal to us when it has passed its peak.

The most important aspect in this discussion is that in the region which we have labelled the bottoming region, *most* shares are either just about to reach their lowest values, or have just risen from their lowest values. The exceptions are those few rogue shares travelling contrary to the market. This region can therefore be considered to be the region of *lowest risk* for *buying* purposes. Conversely, the two regions which have been labelled as 'topping' regions are the regions of *highest risk* for buying. Shares in this region are either about to reach their peaks, and will soon be on their way down, or have already started to decline in price.

Although the rest of this chapter is going to be concerned with how to establish when we are at a market bottom, in order to buy shares, it can also be pointed out that, as far as selling is concerned, we should be aiming for the topping regions. If we miss these for any reason, then we should tend to hold on rather than sell at a bottom region because shares are then poised for an increase in price. However, if the rules outlined in the chapter on selling are adhered to closely, there will be no question of being caught holding shares in a declining market. We will be just about completely in cash, and probably hoping for a heavy fall in prices in order to buy back in at much cheaper levels.

TIMING OF MARKET TURNING POINTS

It is never possible to know at the time that the market has reached its lowest or highest value for the time being. If you rely on the financial press to inform you of the fact, you will be woefully wrong. If the market is in a falling phase, then on the day which later proves to have been the market bottom, the City pages will convince you that there is a long way down to go yet, a further fall of 100 points is on the cards and the holocaust is just around the corner. On the other hand, when the market has been rising for some time, the press will be full of optimism, the index apparently has at least another 100 points rise in it, and all signals are at go. How, therefore, are we to reach any conclusion about the top or bottom of the market? The answer is that we can only do this some time after the event. The later we are in deciding positively that such a day was the point at which the market turned upwards after its long fall, the more we are going to be scooped by investors who woke up to that fact before we did. Thus our potential for profit will be severely limited — in fact by the time commission etc. is taken into account, we may well end up with no profit. On the other hand, if we decide too soon that the market has turned up, and we make a large commitment, we may be wrong and suffer a loss of the capital which we have invested.

It is impossible to predict the stock market with any certainty, but we can learn from the lessons of the past. As we said earlier, we are most concerned with knowing when the market has passed its bottom, and is in a strong recovery, and conversely knowing when it has passed its peak and is on the way down. What we need is a system of rules that indicate, and have been successful in doing this in the past, when the market has turned. If we look again at the Index for the last 10 years or so, in Fig. 5.2 we can identify several points which may be called bottoms. They occurred in mid-1970, late 1974, late 1976 and early 1979. These are the points following which the greatest profits were to be made, since they were usually followed by spectacular rises of some 200 points or so in the Index. It was also still possible to make lesser profits out of less obvious bottoms, which were followed by more minor rises, such as those at the end of 1968, mid-1972, early 1973, mid-1975, mid-1977 and early 1978, even though these rises are for the most part superimposed on the downward part of a wave. Since these minor ripples are of much shorter duration than the waves, being of perhaps a few weeks' to a few months' duration, compared with a year or more for the waves, the timing of an investment to take advantage of these ripples is of much more critical than timing of a wave. We can afford to lose a few weeks at the start of a new wave before we start to invest in selected shares, but to lose the same amount of time with a ripple introduces an unacceptable risk.

We can at this point define two types of investor. Firstly, the less aggressive type, who wishes to keep the risk involved with his investment down to a minimum; secondly, the aggressive investor, who is willing to take more risk in order to make larger profits. The first type should only be prepared to take advantage of the waves, ignoring the minor ripples, while the second type of investor can consider using the ripples as a means of increasing his profit. Note that the aggressive investor will also make a larger profit out of waves, since the start of the wave appears as a ripple, triggering the aggressive investor into action, while the less aggressive investor waits a bit longer until he is sure that a large wave is in the process of formation.

These two types of investor are going to require two slightly different approaches or rules for timing a new investment, although both are based on the same system of plotting *moving averages* of the Friday closing values of the FT Index. To calculate these averages more frequently than at the end of each week only results in wasted effort, since perfectly adequate results are obtained with weekly calculations.

MOVING AVERAGES

We have already pointed out earlier that a plot of the FT Index over the last 12 years consists of three trends, long term, medium term (waves) and short term (ripples). By a simple mathematical technique, which only depends upon the ability to add, subtract and divide, it is possible to separate the long term from the other trends, the medium term from the short term and weekly variations, and the short term from the weekly variations. It is analogous to 'sandpapering' the overall graph in Fig. 5.2. By using a coarse sandpaper we would end up with a gently rising line, which would be the overall long-term trend. Using a medium grade sandpaper, we would remove the jagged ripples, and be left with the waves of a couple of years or so duration. Finally, a fine sandpaper would remove the weekly variations and leave us with the short term ripples.

Since our aim is to make profits within a realistic time span, rather than have to wait 5 years or so for them to mature, we will ignore long-term trends and concentrate upon medium and short-term trends — the waves and ripples we have already mentioned. Thus we will only use medium and fine sandpaper on our graph. The fine sandpaper will be the calculation of a 5-week moving average, while the medium sandpaper will be a 13-week moving average of the FT Index weekly closing price. A 5-week average is what it says it is: the average value of the index over the previous 5 weeks, and can be calculated by adding up the five values for the last 5 weeks and dividing by 5. Similarly, a 13-week average is calculated by adding up the values of the index over the last 13 weeks and dividing by 13. The adjective 'moving' is in a sense superfluous, since all it means is that our average is changing each week, which it will normally do when we compare this week's values with last week's.

Rather than, each week, adding together the previous 13 weeks values before we divide by 13, we can simplify things if we keep a note of the total for the previous 13 weeks before we divide it by 13. Then, the following week all we have to do is add the new week's value to this total, and subtract the value of the index for the 14th week back. Dividing this new total by 13 gives us the new value of the 13-week average. A similar approach can be made to calculate the 5-week moving average, only this time we add the new week's value and subtract the 6th week back from the running total. The whole thing should be clear from Table 5.2.

The total of the first 5 weeks' values of the FT Index is 2295.9, entered in the 5 week total column. Divided by 5 this gives a 5-week average of 459.2. The

Table 5.2. Calculation of 5- and 13-week moving averages of the FT Index

Date	Index	5-week average			13-week average		
		Subtract	Total	Average	Subtract	Total	Average
18.3.78	457.2	X			X		
25.3.78	460.5	X			X		
1.4.78	463.8	X					
8.4.78	467.0	X					
15.4.78	447.4	X	2295.9	459.2			
22.4.78	454.0	X	2292.7	458.5			
28.4.78	465.7	X	2297.9	459.6			
5.5.78	481.5	X	2315.6	463.1			
13.5.78	488.3	X	2336.9	467.4			
20.5.78	470.6		2360.1	472.0			
27.5.78	476.1		2382.2	476.4			
2.6.78	475.5		2392.0	478.4			
9.6.78	466.9		2377.4	475.5		6074.5	467.3
16.6.78	470.6		2359.7	471.9		6087.9	468.3

next week, the new value of 454.0 is added to this total, while the 6th week back value (457.2) is subtracted. This gives a new total of 2292.7 which is divided by 5 to give a five-week average of 458.5. In order to avoid confusion on which value is to be subtracted, we put a cross in the 'subtract' column opposite the value which we have just subtracted. Thus, the following week we know that the value following the one with a cross is the one to be subtracted.

We cannot compute a 13-week average, of course, until we have 13 weeks' values of the Index. Then we can proceed in the same way as we did for the 5-week average, but of course dividing the 13-week running totals by 13, and putting a cross in the 13 week 'subtract' column so as not to lose track of the value to be subtracted the following week.

After a time we will have a list of values of the Index itself, the 5-week moving average and the 13-week moving average. We will be able to see at a glance whether the 5-week average and 13-week average are both moving up, both moving down or one going up and one going down. Although some people have the ability to extract a great deal of information from long columns of figures, it is easier to see what is going on, and has more impact, if these figures are plotted on a graph, since the various wave formations will then stand out clearly. To show the sandpapering effect of these moving averages on the weekly values of the index, separate graphs of the Index, the 5-week moving average and the 13-week moving average are shown in Fig. 5.5.

We now come to an important point about moving averages which has frequently been ignored in books about share movements which have displayed such averages (usually a 200-day one) on top of graphs of weekly or daily prices. This point is that the average of a number of weekly prices has to be associated with the middle of the number of weeks taken. In the table which earlier showed how to calculate these averages, we put the values for both the 5-week and 13-week averages opposite the last weekly price that we had used. This is perfectly fine if we are just using the table to tell us *when* the average has changed from a down direction to an up direction but we cannot put these three values, weekly, 5-week average and 13-week average on the same week's position on a graph. So, the 5-week average has to be plotted 3 weeks back in time, i.e. the middle week of the 5-week span and the 13-week average has to be plotted 7 weeks back, the middle of a 13-week span. Figure 5.6 shows the three graphs from Fig. 5.5 displayed on the same grid. For the reasons we have been discussing, the 5-week average terminates 3 weeks before, and the 13-week average 7 weeks before the end of the weekly price points. Figure 5.5 emphasizes an aspect that is lost if the averages are not plotted with this time lag — the weekly price oscillates about the 5-week average, which in turn oscillates about the 13-week average. As we will discuss in the final chapter, the larger the number of weeks used to compute an average, the smoother the resulting curve will be and the easier it will be to predict it forward into the future. Knowing that these various averages oscillate about each other makes it easier to predict price ranges for shares and so correctly plotted moving averages have a very useful predictive value.

In order to avoid confusion, we shall continue to *calculate* the averages exactly

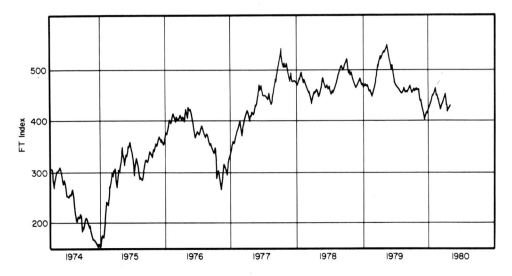

Figure 5.5(a). The movements of the Financial Times Index weekly closing values since 1974. The Index is plotted on a linear scale.

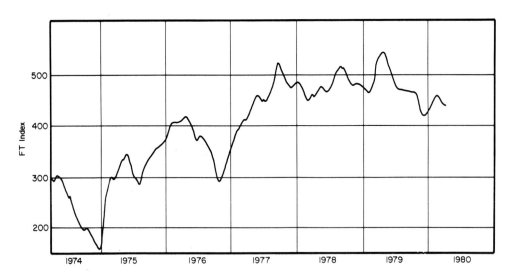

Figure 5.5(b). The 5-week moving average of the weekly closing values of the Financial Times Index since 1974.

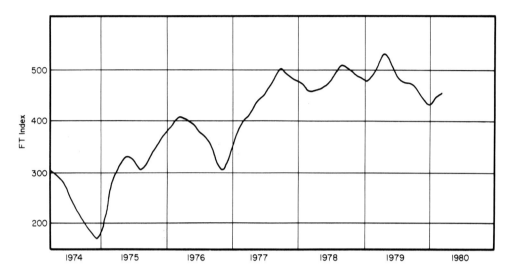

Figure 5.5(c). The 13-week moving average of the weekly closing values of the Financial Times Index since 1974.

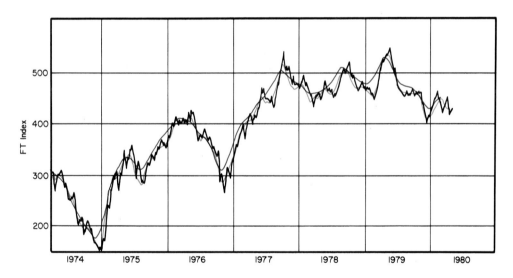

Figure 5.6. The relationship between the weekly closing values of the Financial Times Index (black), the 5-week moving average (green) and the 13-week moving average (red).

as shown in Table 5.2, since in this chapter we are almost exclusively interested in *when* the averages signal that they have changed direction; which we interpret as meaning the market has changed direction. Whenever the averages are plotted on a graph, however, they will always be plotted with the appropriate time lag. Thus, when we want, for historical reasons, to retrieve from a graph of moving averages the actual dates when at the time we would have seen the average change direction, we have to *add* the appropriate time lag to the date the averages reached a maximum or minimum on the graph.

Now, the question is, how are these moving averages going to help us to decide that it is time to make an investment? The answer is most clearly illustrated by reference to the graph of the 13-week moving average. There are five points at which the average changes direction from down to up and these occur in early 1975, late 1975, late 1976, mid-1978 and early 1979. If you look at the same points on the more complex graph of the Index itself, you can see that the Index then rose by very large amounts, of the order of a couple of hundred points. So a turn up in the 13-week moving average has, in the recent past, acted as a signal to tell us that a considerable rise in the market has just started, and that it is time for us to get invested in order to take advantage of the coming rise.

Well, what about the 5-week average? A closer look of its picture shows that the 5-week average also changed from down to up at about the same points that the 13-week average did, but that, in addition it also turned up a few times for a short time on occasions when the 13-week average did not. In other words, the 5-week average can give a false signal that the market is changing to a strong upward trend. If you look at these times of a false signal on the graph of the Index itself, it will be noticed that even so, there was still a small rise in the Index, which usually only lasted a few weeks, but this is still enough either to make a small profit or to limit the loss to a small one provided one is prepared to sell out a few weeks later when it becomes obvious that the signal is false because the 13-week average does not turn up.

It is difficult to see, because of the large time-scale in Fig. 5.5, the small time differences between a turn up in the Index itself, a turn up in the 5-week average and a turn up in the 13-week average. In order to get over this problem, in Table 5.3 are shown these three values for a few weeks either side of the turning points mentioned earlier in 1975, 1976, 1978 and 1979.

From the figures in Table 5.3 it can be seen that the 5-week average is more volatile than the 13-week average, that is, it reacts more quickly than the latter to a change in the direction of the market from falling to rising. For example, in the market bottom during December 1974/January 1975, the lowest value of the weekly index was achieved on 27th December. The 5-week average turned up on 10th January, and the 13-week average turned up 2 weeks later on 24th January. The Index itself rose some 80 points between 17th and 24th January and then a further 100 points or so during the next few months. So an investor who jumped the gun and invested when the 5-week average turned up on 10th January made a considerably larger profit than one who waited 2 weeks longer.

Sometimes there is a gap of several weeks between the turning up of the 5-week average and the 13-week average. The market bottom which occurred in

October/November 1976 is a case in point. From Table 5.3 it can be seen that the Index reached its lowest point on 29th October and the 5-week average turned up 2 weeks later, on 12th November. It was not until 31st December that the 13-week index turned up. The Index itself climbed about 80 points during the period between the two signals. There was still plenty of profit left in the situation, because by the following September the Index climbed to a then record high of just short of 550.

Table 5.3. Behaviour of weekly closing values of the FT Index and the 5-week and 13-week moving averages of weekly closing values of the Index at major market bottoms

Market bottom	Date	FT Index*	5-week average	13-week average
December 1974/	29 Nov. 74	165	175	190
January 1975	6 Dec. 74	160	168	185
	13 Dec. 74	150	162	181
	20 Dec. 74	161	160	179
	27 Dec. 74	147	157	176
	3 Jan. 75	150	154	173
	10 Jan. 75	175	157	170
	17 Jan. 75	170	158	168.
	26 Jan. 75	252	178	172
	31 Jan. 75	230	195	175
	7 Feb. 75	275	220	182
August 1975	11 July 75	330	316	333
	18 July 75	296	307	329
	25 July 75	285	298	325
	1 Aug. 75	290	298	324
	8 Aug. 75	287	292	320
	15 Aug. 75	280	282	316
	22 Aug. 75	295	282	312
	29 Aug. 75	310	287	309
	5 Sept. 75	326	294	306
	12 Sept. 75	318	301	304
	19 Sept. 75	343	313	305
October 1976	1 Oct. 76	322	341	361
	8 Oct. 76	287	328	353
	15 Oct. 76	305	321	346
	22 Oct. 76	285	310	339
	29 Oct. 76	264	293	331
	5 Nov. 76	281	285	324
	12 Nov. 76	308	289	319
	19 Nov. 76	318	292	316
	26 Nov. 76	294	294	311
	3 Dec. 76	295	300	307
	10 Dec. 76	324	308	306
	17 Dec. 76	331	313	305

Table 5.3. *(cont'd)*

Market bottom	Date	FT Index*	5-week average	13-week average
October 1976	24 Dec. 76	345	332	308
	31 Dec. 76	365	332	308
March – April	3 Feb. 78	471	483	478
1978	10 Feb. 78	456	474	477
	17 Feb. 78	459	470	477
	24 Feb. 78	445	462	474
	3 Mar. 78	436	453	471
	10 Mar. 78	459	451	469
	17 Mar. 78	451	451	468
	24 Mar. 78	461	452	467
	31 Mar. 78	464	455	465
	7 Apr. 78	467	461	463
	14 Apr. 78	447	459	460
	21 Apr. 78	454	458	457
	28 Apr. 79	466	460	457
	5 May 78	482	463	457
	12 May 78	488	467	460
February 1979	19 Jan. 79	479	476	479
	26 Jan. 79	465	474	477
	2 Feb. 79	467	473	476
	9 Feb. 79	451	467	475
	16 Feb. 79	455	463	473
	23 Feb. 79	461	461	472
	2 Mar. 79	485	465	472
	9 Mar. 79	515	474	474
	16 Mar. 79	511	486	476
	23 Mar. 79	535	502	480

*To nearest whole number.

The two averages of the FT Index and the Index itself are plotted on graphs for each of these five bottoms in Fig. 5.6. We can see how the bottoms in the Index and in each of the two averages now almost overlap and it is also evident that the weekly index values oscillate about the averages.

The dates at which the 5-week averages and 13-week averages signalled a rise in the market are given in Table 5.4. As we have mentioned, since the beginning of 1974, the 13-week average has changed direction from down to up five times and each time the market has shown a considerable rise. In fact, we could go back even further to the end of the war in 1945 and the same thing is true about the 13-week average, so that we can conclude that in future any turn up in the 13-week average has a high probability of being correct in signalling a considerable rise in share prices.

There is no such high probability attached to a change from down to up in the direction of the 5-week moving average, as can be seen from Table 5.4. Of 16 signals given between the beginning of 1974 and September 1979, seven were incorrect and nine were correct. On those occasions where a change in the 5-week average has been a correct signal for a market rise, confirmed by a turn up in the 13-week average, the great advantage of it has been the earlier opportunity to get into the market. We can see from Table 5.4 that on such occasions the turn up in the 5-week average precedes that in the 13-week average by anything from 1 to 6 weeks.

Table 5.4. Market rises signalled by 5-week and 13-week averages since 1974 and whether correct or not

5-week average signals			*13-week average signals*		
	1974			1974	
3 May		wrong		none	
26 July		wrong			
25 October		wrong			
	1975			1975	
10 January		right	24 January		right
4 April		wrong	19 September		right
29 August		right			
	1976			1976	
2 July		wrong	31 December		right
12 November		right			
	1977			1977	
5 August		right		none	
23 December		right			
	1978			1978	
24 February		right	5 May		right
28 April		right			
14 July		right			
8 December		wrong			
	1979			1979	
2 March		right	9 March		right
17 August		wrong			

Since, as has been pointed out, the 5-week moving average sometimes gives a false signal, in the sense that the market does then not move upwards for a lengthy period but only for a few weeks, then it will be more appropriate for an aggressive investor to take advantage of such a situation, while the less aggressive investor is more temperamentally suited to waiting until the bull market is confirmed by the 13-week average. It is important to decide into which category you should put yourself.

AGGRESSIVE AND CAUTIOUS INVESTORS

By definition, the cautious investor is a person who is less willing to take risks than an aggressive investor. He will take a bit more time to be convinced that the market is moving ahead and that it is time to buy his selected shares. Because of this longer period of time necessary to take an investment decision, he will necessarily make less profit out of the changed condition of the market than an aggressive investor who has acted a few weeks earlier. He will have to pay higher prices for his shares because prices will have been moving ahead during those crucial weeks. On the other hand, the more cautious investor may score on those occasions when the market has given a false indication that it has changed direction for the better. He is able to stand back and watch his more adventurous colleagues take losses, unless they are prepared to admit to themselves that they have made a mistake and decide to close out their positions.

It is important to know yourself psychologically, since to act aggressively when one is fundamentally cautious can lead to a number of sleepless nights worrying about the size of the commitment you have made. Investment under these conditions ceases to be the source of pleasure it ought to be and becomes a source of tension. There is even a category of people who worry unduly even when following the rules outlined for the more cautious investor. Such people should avoid the stock market entirely and concentrate upon the other forms of investment discussed in the opening chapter of this book. As a general rule, at least until one has gained more experience in investment, if a particular holding becomes a source of worry it should be reduced to levels at which you can come to terms with the uncertainty. If you cannot do this, it is probably best to close out the entire holding in that security.

A further point at which individual investor psychology comes into play is in selling a particular holding, especially if it has only been held for a short time. Some investors consider that to sell is some sort of confession of failure. Nothing could be further from the truth. A decision to buy is based upon all the knowledge available at the time of buying. Conditions may well change a week later for that particular security so that it then becomes a bad holding. To sell then is not a confession of failure, but an indication that you have been alert to the changed circumstances and their implication for your particular holding. The fact to bear in mind at all times is that your capital has been hard come by and that your aim is to increase it or preserve it. Cutting adrift from a losing situation may not increase your capital but is certainly preserving it for investment elsewhere under more favourable conditions.

The Cautious Investor

The key to investment decisions by a cautious investor will be the movement of the 13-week moving average. Once this turns up from its downward trend the probability is that we can look forward to many months of a steadily rising market and provided the correct choice of shares has been made, a large increase in capital will occur. It is essential to become fully invested within a few weeks of this turn up in the 13-week average, otherwise the largest slice of profits, which normally occurs at the beginning of a new bull market, will be missed. As discussed later, the choice of investments will have usually narrowed itself down to about four or five shares, since to be invested in more results in too thin a spread, with possible reduction in profits, as well as being difficult to keep fully abreast of at all times.

There is something to be said for spreading the investment in each particular share over a period of 2 or 3 weeks, buying, say, one-third of the envisaged holding at a time, and not buying the next third until the price has moved up. This, of course, results in an average price for the share that is higher than if the complete holding had been bought at the beginning, but as long as the price is rising during the period, this average price will be less than the market price. This means that at all times there will be a profit locked into the situation, which hopefully will not be allowed to trickle away. If the price does not rise shortly after the initial investment, due to unforeseen circumstances, we then have two-thirds of the anticipated sum left to invest in our other choices which should be doing much better.

Although the turn up in the 13-week moving average is the trigger for the cautious investor, the 5-week average can be used as an early warning device that the 13-week average may shortly move upwards. Thus he should be following both averages closely and as soon as the 5-week turns up, he can finalize his choice of shares in readiness for the change in direction of the 13-week moving average, should it occur.

The Aggressive Investor

The aggressive investor is willing to increase the risk inherent in making an investment in order to increase his profits. Thus he needs a signal which is more volatile than the 13-week average and tells him more quickly than the latter that the bottom of the market has probably been passed, but with less certainty than the signal from the 13-week average (certainty is less because something has to be traded for the gain in time). The 5-week moving average fulfils the requirement of the aggressive investor, but, as mentioned before, and as can be seen from the plot of the 5-week average in Figs 5.5 and 5.6, there are a number of occasions when this average turns up only for a short time and is not followed by the 13-week average.

Both the correct and incorrect signals of the 5-week moving average have already been given in Table 5.4, where we showed that there were nine correct and seven incorrect signals. Therefore there is not much better than an even chance that a turn up in the 5-week average is indicating the start of a bull market. This may appear to be something of a gamble, but several points should be borne in mind. Firstly, even if the indication is false, there may be an opportunity to make a small profit by selling a week or so after buying, because prices will rise for a short time, at least in those securities which have been chosen because of their potential gain. Secondly, if a profit is not forthcoming, the loss should be minimal provided the position is sold out when it is realized that a bull market is not commencing. Thirdly, although the chances of the 5-week average indicating the start of a bull market are about evens, the chances of a profit are very much greater than this, since if it is the start of a new bull market, the profits are going to be very large indeed, whereas, if it is not, the loss will be small, being limited by the fact that you sell out. The professionals may well use the terms 'upside potential' and 'downside potential' in this situation. When the 5-week moving average turns up, the upside potential is greater than the downside potential.

It must be emphasized again, however, that this is only true if the aggressive investor is prepared to recognize that he may well have to sell a holding shortly after he has acquired it if the market has given a false indication. Failure to do this may result in such losses that a good proportion of the rise during the eventual bull market will be offset by them.

The rules discussed above can be restated simply as follows:

1. While the 5-week and 13-week moving averages are falling, do not buy shares.
2. When the 5-week average turns up, with the 13-week average falling, the aggressive investor can buy, but be prepared to sell soon if the 5-week average turns down again and the 13-week average continues to fall.
3. When the 13-week average turns up the cautious investor can now buy within the next few weeks. The aggressive investor now knows he was right!

Chapter 6

What to Buy

The next most important decision after deciding when to buy is what to buy and this chapter is concerned with the development of selection procedures. Although, eventually, certain shares are recommended for buying, the recommendation or otherwise of shares does not imply praise or criticism of those companies or the way in which the companies are managed. The selections are based entirely on the movement of the share prices.

As pointed out in the last chapter, when the market turns up in a new bull phase, almost all equities rise in value. So, provided we have a reasonable spread of investments in our portfolio, our portfolio will also gain. It is correct timing that virtually guarantees a profit. The size of the profit, however, will depend upon which equities we have bought. A badly selected portfolio may appreciate by only a few per cent during a roaring bull market, and nothing is more galling than to see your shares left behind in the general stampede upwards. On the other hand, a properly selected portfolio will be at the front of the stampede, and you may easily see the value of your holding double in the course of a few months.

The magnitude of the problem in choosing shares to buy is easily grasped by a quick glance at the back pages of the *Financial Times*. The list of equities quoted on the London Stock Exchange covers nearly two whole pages, 12 columns in all. So, how are we to select the winners from this bewildering variety of shares? One way of looking at this problem might be to decide that somebody, somewhere, in the past has already reduced this large list down to 30 shares in the form of the 'blue chip' companies which form the FT 30 Index. After all, these are considered to be the backbone of British industry, and so we would think that we cannot go far wrong by investing in these. In support of this approach is the fact that in the last chapter, we showed that we could determine, with a high probability, the point in time at which the Index, i.e. these 30 companies, would show a large rise of the order of 100 to 200 points. Although 'buying the Index' is a feasible proposition, we can put forward a number of good reasons for not adopting this approach to investment in equities.

The first of these is the large cost, as far as the small private investor is concerned. The smallest investment in each share is going to be of the order of £100 to £200, if buying costs are to be kept to a reasonable minimum. Because of this, only investors who can splash out £3000 to £6000 are in a position to undertake this exercise.

A second reason is the difficulty in giving the amount of attention to such a large portfolio that is necessary if it is to be managed properly. All through this book, the theme is that investment should not be an onerous task and that a portfolio of not more than six shares is probably the best size for the person with limited spare time available. With 30 shares to follow each week, it would be difficult to reach clear-headed decisions about selling individual holdings when it is necessary to do so. There will be a tendency to allow longer and longer time intervals to elapse between evaluations of the situation. As shown in the next chapter, this can be an expensive failing, since prices, even of blue chip companies, can fall dramatically in the course of a week or two.

A third factor, which is very important, and perhaps not so obvious, is that the profit potential of the Index itself is fairly limited. Even in a roaring bull phase, the Index is unlikely to rise by more than 20 – 30%. Although a 100 point rise looks spectacular, percentage-wise it only represents 20% if it occurs when the Index is already at 500. Of course, as pointed out earlier, because of the way in which it is constructed, the constituents of the Index do slightly better than the Index itself, but even so, this only makes a small difference and the fact remains that we are unlikely to make large profits out of these 30 companies. It is, of course, important to make large profits when the Index is rising, because these have to make up for those other occasions when the market is falling and we are not invested.

It is of interest to see what profit we would have made if we *had* invested in the 30 companies of the FT Index on 5th May 1978. This date is chosen because the 13-week moving average for 1978 signalled a market rise during the first week of May by changing from a downward trend to an upward trend at that time. The Index itself ended the week at 481.5. One year later, the day after the General Election, the Index reached a then all-time high of 558.6 on 4th May 1979. The gain in the Index over the year was therefore 16%. Table 6.1 shows the prices of the shares of the constituent companies on those dates and the percentage gain (or loss) of these during the period. The gain in these companies' shares over the year was 17.3%, slightly more than the gain in the Index itself.

An alternative to investing in all 30 of these companies is, of course, to select just six or less of their number. This would overcome the objections of the large cost involved in buying into all 30 and would also give us a portfolio of manageable size. The problem is, unfortunately, that we have no means of deciding which of the 30 are going to do best during the following year. We may, through good luck or judgement, happen upon the six which do the best, which in the case of those in Table 6.1 would have been John Brown, GEC, Grand Metropolitan, British Petroleum, Blue Circle Cement and Imperial Group. This would have made us an average gain of 56.2% over the year.

On the other hand, of course, we might through bad luck just pick on the worst performers, which would have been EMI, P & O, Marks & Spencer, Glaxo, Turner & Newall and Courtaulds. In such a case, we would have made an average loss of 13.3% during the year. In fact, since seven of the 30 shares actually declined during 1978/79, there is about a one in four chance that any share picked at random would be a loser and a better than even chance that there would be at least one loser among any six selected at random.

Table 6.1. Price movement of the shares of the FT 30 constituent companies during the year 5 May 78 to 4 May 79

Share	Price at 5 May 78	Price at 4 May 79	% gain (loss)	Share	Price at 5 May 78	Price at 4 May 78	% gain (loss)
Allied Brew.	93.5	102	9.1	Grand Met.	113	179	58.4
Beecham	664	725	9.2	GKN	284	308	8.4
Blue Circle	252	342	35.7	Hawker S.	214	266	24.3
BOC	75	81	8.0	ICI	358	414	15.6
Boots	210	235	11.9	Imperial	79.5	107	34.6
Bowater	203	209	3.0	London Br.	70	72	2.9
BP	824	1230	49.3	Lucas	300	310	3.3
J.Brown	324	587	81.2	M & S	147	130	(11.6)
Cad. Schwep.	53	69	30.2	P & O	99	86	(13.0)
Courtaulds	124	116	(6.5)	Plessey	98	107	9.2
Distillers	186	249	33.9	Tate & Lyle	190	156	17.9
Dunlop	81	80	(1.2)	Tube Inv.	374	436	16.6
EMI	144	114	(20.8)	Turner & N.	176	166	(5.7)
GEC	253	450	77.8	UDS	94	121	29.8
Glaxo	565	515	(8.8)	Vickers	182	210	15.4

Average gain 17.3%

Having decided that investing in all, or just a few of the shares of the companies comprising the FT 30 Index is either too big a task, or unlikely to yield us a large profit, then we have to find some other way of selecting shares. Of course, this other way has to be an improvement on the FT 30 list, otherwise we would be better off, in spite of the disadvantages just pointed out, in investing in a small number of shares chosen from the FT 30 constituents. So, each time we reduce the list of shares down from the initial number as listed on the back pages of the *Financial Times*, we will have to check that the performance of the reduced list is superior to that of the FT 30 companies.

The most obvious way of choosing shares is by selecting them at random from all those possible. This could be done by, for example, throwing 30 darts at the relevant pages of the *Financial Times*. This may sound foolish but the interesting point emerges that we are likely to do better by doing this than by investing in some or all of the FT 30 shares. This is because, perhaps surprisingly, the constituents of the FT 30 Index did not perform as well as the whole market during the year commencing 5th May 1978. We have already pointed out that the FT Index rose from 481.5 to 558.6, a gain of 16%, while the constituent shares gained 17.3%. The All Share Index, covering 750 shares, rose from 216.28 to 283.82 during the year, for a gain of 31.2%. This fact might lead us to question the idea of a 'blue chip' company, if such a company's shares do not consistently perform as well as the rest of the market. Quite obviously we are better off by avoiding them — as long as we do not all rush out and try to sell them at the same time! Since the market as a whole has of late performed better than the market in the FT 30 shares, a more rigorous check on the performance of any group of shares which we choose from the whole market would be to require them to do better than the whole market. Thus, at least for the present time period, any such list would in any case outperform the shares of the FT 30 constituents.

So, from now on, as far as selecting shares is concerned, our yardstick for choosing a list of shares for the period in question will be the All Share Index gain of 31.2%. There are a number of criteria we can apply to shorten the large number of shares down to manageable proportions, but each time we apply such a selection procedure, it has to result in an improved gain over the year for our shorter list. The first selection we make must give a list with a gain of better than the whole market's gain of 31.2%. A further point about the selection procedures is that they should be fairly simple to carry out and the simplest would be based entirely upon considerations of the movements in the share prices themselves. We want simplicity, because, as we have pointed out before, we have to make the whole business of investment fairly undemanding in terms of our time. If we are going to consider company profits, the latest news about particular companies, and other types of fundamental data, we will soon be swamped with the demands of keeping up with this vast amount of information. If we are able to demonstrate that we can achieve good results just from a consideration of the share prices, without having to keep up with all the other data, then we can accept this as being a satisfactory situation in terms of the return for our effort.

We can put forward, at least as a start, two criteria which would, superficially, appear sensible ways of spotlighting those shares which we expect to do well. We can then test each of these criteria for effectiveness, as discussed above, in choosing shares which outperform the rest of the market.

1. Larger profits can be made out of shares which have a history of fluctuating widely in price, i.e. which can be considered to be volatile shares.
2. Larger profits can be made out of shares which have not declined as much as the market in general prior to the start of the latest bull market.

VOLATILE SHARES

As far as volatility is concerned, it would seem obvious that if we are after a large profit, it makes no sense to invest in shares whose price historically has moved within a narrow range. On the other hand, shares which move over a wide range each year have the potential to make us large profits. The pessimist may well argue that they have the potential to make us a large loss, which is of course true if one neglects proper timing of the investment. Provided we buy at the correct time, which can be determined as we showed in the last chapter, the risk of loss is minimized. An actual example would serve to show the potential for profit by investing in such a share. The yearly price ranges for the engineering company Babcock & Wilcox Ltd (now called Babcock International) are shown in Fig. 6.1. Before going into detail, some general comments can be made about the presentation of share charts. The price scale on such charts is almost always presented as a logarithmic scale, rather than the linear scale such as we used in displaying movements in the FT 30 Index. These scales have the property that a percentage change in the price covers the same vertical distance irrespective of the starting price. Thus the distance between 20p and 40p is the same as the distance between 30p and 60p (100% increase in both instances). This would not be true of course for a linear scale, the distance between 30p and 60p being half as much again as that between 20p and 40p. Where we are interested in profit, which is best expressed as a percentage, we can more easily gauge this from a logarithmic chart than a linear one but for a prediction of price movements, a linear scale is usually advantageous. Hence both are used in this book, depending on the aspect of investment being discussed.

In the case of Babcock & Wilcox, the logarithmic scale means that bars of the

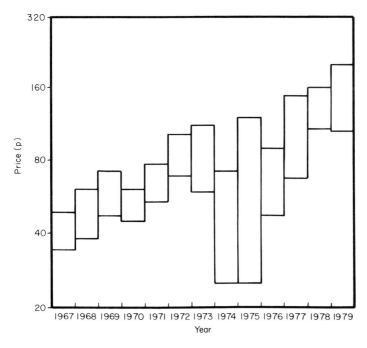

Figure 6.1. Yearly price ranges of share of Babcock and Wilcox since 1967. Prices are on a logarithmic scale.

same length would indicate the same percentage change or degree of volatility. It can be seen that the length of the bars, and hence the volatility, has tended to increase since the late 1960s, implying that Babcock & Wilcox shares are now fluctuating each year more widely than previously. Of course, this tendency may well reverse in the future.

Although the advantage of such a chart is in its simplicity in depicting price ranges, we must not be misled into thinking that such an amount of profit is available each year. This is because the chart does not show *when* the extremes of the price range were reached. To see that, one has to look at a chart of the weekly closing prices over a period of time. Such a chart for Babcock & Wilcox is given in Chapter 7. The shares may well have started the year at a high and ended the year at a low. In a sense, therefore, the chart also shows the potential for loss as well as profit. What is obvious from the chart is that to date the high for each year has always been higher than the low for the preceding year. So, even if we neglect the fact that for about half of the years shown in Fig. 6.1 it would be possible to buy at the low and sell at the high *within* the same year, we can look at the less advantageous case of buying at one year's low and selling at the following year's high just to gain some idea of the possible profit. If we were able to buy exactly at the highs and lows, we would achieve a very large profit, as shown in Table 6.2.

A person who started with £100 invested in Babcock & Wilcox in 1967, and continued to buy and sell, reinvesting the proceeds at the exact lows and highs would have ended with an investment worth £4600 in 1978! As pointed out above, the actual gain would have been many times higher than this because extra transactions could have been carried out in some of the in-between years where the low preceded the high.

Of course, the above calculation is theoretical, because no one is going to be able to buy exactly at the bottom and sell exactly at the top consistently. What we can hope for, however, is that we can get fairly near to those positions, say within 5 or 10% of the lows and highs.

It should be pointed out that because of this difficulty of determining the exact points of the highs and lows in share prices, we will make almost no profit out of buying and selling shares which only move 20% or so between their low

Table 6.2. The results of transactions in Babcock & Wilcox shares since 1967 at peak highs and lows

Year bought	Year sold	Price bought	Price sold	% gain
1967	1968	34	59	70
1969	1970	48	59 ⅜	25
1971	1972	55 ⅜	105 ½	90
1973	1974	60	74	23
1975	1976	25	92	290
1977	1978	70	165	140
			Cumulative gain	4500

and high point. For example, if a share fluctuates between a low price of 150p and a high price of 180p, i.e. a gain of 20%, then being realistic, we are unlikely to buy at better than 155 to 160p and sell at 170 to 175p. Thus our profit, excluding buying and selling costs, will only be of the order of 10 to 20p, which is about 7 to 14% depending upon the exact prices involved. If we carry out the 'round trip' of buying and selling over a short period of time so that no dividend is received to offset commissions etc., then our profit will be of the order of 0 to 7% or so. Because of this, it is crucial to deal in shares which are going to swing much more than 20% between their highs and lows.

To show how this real life situation would change the theoretical gains given in Table 6.2, we can make the assumption that we can get to within 10% of the buying and selling prices of Babcock & Wilcox. So, the buying and selling prices at which we would probably have bought, and the resulting profits, are given in Table 6.3.

The cumulative gain of 1187% obtained by buying and selling six times since 1967 is high by any standards, and represents an average gain of about 65% for each transaction, reinforcing the case for investing in volatile shares.

Since we are advocating the purchase of volatile shares, we may well ask how volatile UK shares are on the whole. This can be gauged from Fig. 6.2, in which the percentage movement from their low values are given for 500 shares in 1978. These shares were chosen on a random basis, so that they give a fair representation of the market as a whole. It can be seen that very few shares moved less than 20% from their low values, and very few moved more than about 160%. There were some extremely volatile shares which moved between a factor of five and ten times their low values, but since these are few and atypical, they are not shown on the figure. The 'average' share showed a movement of between 20 and 50% from its low value during the year, so that we can define volatile shares for our purposes as being shares which moved more than the average, say 70% and upwards.

Having shown the advantage possible when investing in a volatile share, it now remains to be shown that in general such shares are going to give a better result than the market as a whole. We can do this by considering a list of such shares based upon their highs and lows for the preceding year, the list being

Table 6.3. The results of transactions in Babcock & Wilcox shares since 1967 at probable buying and selling prices

Year bought	Year sold	Price bought	Price sold	% gain
1967	1968	37	53	43
1969	1970	53	53	0
1971	1972	60	94	56
1973	1974	66	67	1
1975	1976	28	83	196
1977	1978	77	149	93
			Cumulative gain	1187

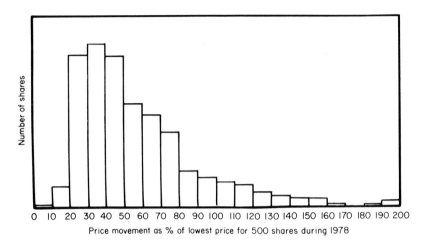

Figure 6.2. Volatility of UK shares. The histogram, derived from a total of 500 shares, shows the number of shares in categories of movements from under 10 to 200%.

constructed during the early part of 1978, a time when the market in general was falling. The downward trend of the market was confirmed by the fact that the 5-week and 13-week moving averages of the FT Index were both falling.

The list of shares given in Table 6.4, 118 in all, was chosen so as to be fairly representative in numbers of the various sectors of the market, such as electrical, engineering, food etc. The high and low values for the previous year at the time of compilation of the list are given under the heading '1977/78 low, high'. The volatility of the shares is represented by the ratio of the high to the low price for the year 1977/78. In this table, the least volatile share is Grand Metropolitan, with a high/low ratio of 1.76, while the most volatile is Automated Security, with a ratio of 10.7. Since the buy signal was given during the first week in May 1978, the price of these shares is given on 5th May 1978, as is the price on 16th September 1978 — the week during which the market reached a temporary high of about 530, and the price on 4th May 1979, i.e. 1 year after the shares would have been purchased for this exercise.

The average gain on these shares for the year was 48.4%. This is significantly better than the gain in the FT Index companies (17.3%) and the gain in the All Share Index (31.2%) during the same period of time. So, at least based on the prices for 1978, the potential for profit is improved by selecting shares on the basis of their volatility rather than by just selecting at random from the whole market.

STRONG SHARES

The recent strength of a share is a second consideration in choosing our list of shares to buy. Since we are compiling our list of shares while the market is

Table 6.4. Shares chosen in early 1978 on the basis of volatility: subsequent price movements

Share	1977/78 low	high	Price at 5 May 78		% of 77/78 high	Price at 4 May 79	% gain (loss)
Breweries							
Arthur Bell	79	236	256		108.0	190 xd	(25.8)
Highland Distillers	52	158	143		90.5	102 xd	(28.7)
Whitbread	59	96 ½	99		102.0	147	48.5
					Average gain for sector		2.0%
Building							
Blue Circle	153	294	252		85.7	342 xd	35.7
Bryant	13	55	54		98.2	68 xd	25.9
John Carr	16 ½	48	46		95.8	65	41.3
Comben Group	13	38	31		81.5	40	29.0
Countryside	9	41	40		97.6	68	70.0
D.Crouch	22	99	87		87.9	128	47.0
Crouch Group	23	73	71		97.3	88	23.9
FPA Construction	7	26	23		88.5	13	(43.5)
Federated Land	13	47	46		97.8	79	71.7
Hoveringham	20	64	77	xd	120.3	96	24.7
Johnson-Richards	36	118 ½	130		109.7	166	27.7
London Brick	40	86	70		81.4	78	2.9
Marley	44	98	84		85.7	101	20.2
Monk	23 ¼	86	100		116.3	170	(30.0)
Mowlem	44	143	124	xd	86.7	130	4.8
Newarthill	45	186	150	xd	80.6	270	40.0
Phoenix Timber	64	198	160		80.8	153	(4.4)
UBM	34	79	74 ½		94.3	76	2.0
					Average gain for sector		21.6%
Chemicals, Plastics							
Coalite	43 ¾	78	77		98.7	82	6.5
Rentokil	34	62	58		93.5	118	103.0
Stewart Plastics	74	151	132		87.4	204	(54.5)
					Average gain for sector		54.7%
Stores							
Burton	50	142	126		88.7	347	175
Forminster*	30	91	102		112.4	168	64.7
Homecharm	60	122	148	xd	121.3	380	156.8
Lee Cooper	29 ¼	137	135		98.5	302	123.7
Marks & Spencer	96	173	147		84.9	130	(11.6)
MFI	15 ½	76	78		102.6	380	387.0
Maple	5	17	19		111.8	31 xd	63.0
Ratners	17 ½	112	68		60.7	93	36.8
Austin Reed	32	98	86		87.7	147 xd	70.9
Rosgill	4	13 ½	14		103.7	31	121.4
Selincourt	10 ¾	28	26 ½		94.6	33	24.5

Table 6.4. *(cont'd)*

Share	1977/78 low	high	Price at 5 May 78	% of 77/78 high	Price at 4 May 79	% gain (loss)
Shermans	3	11	12 ½	113.6	14 ½	16.0
Time Products	39	128	136	106.3	249	83.0
UDS	53	99	94	94.9	121	28.7
J.Walker	32	103	86	83.5	132	53.5
				Average gain for sector		92.9%
Electrical						
Automated Sec.	5 ½	59	79 xd	133.8	145 xd	83.5
Cableform	8 ¾	79	66	83.5	77	16.7
Comet Radiovision	29	115	122	106.1	162	32.7
Dubilier	9 ½	18 ½	17 ½	94.6	31 ½	80.0
Electrocomps. *	44	182 ½	199	109.0	312 ½	123.6
Energy Services	4 ¼	14 ¼	11	77.2	30 ¼	175.0
EMI	141	254	144	56.7	114	(20.8)
Laurence Scott	44	136	123	90.4	94	(23.6)
Plessey	62	117	117	83.8	107	8.2
Pye Holdings	38	114	107	93.9	104	(2.8)
United Scientific	92	293	322	109.9	265	(17.7)
Wellco Holdings	9	27	25	92.6	36 ½	46.0
				Average gain for sector		41.7%
Engineering						
Babcock & Wilcox	70	153	128	83.7	198 xd	54.7
Brooks Tool	11	28	32	114.0	48	50.0
John Brown	98	297	324	190.1	587	81.2
Bullough	65	142	125	88.0	270	116.0
Hawker Siddeley	113	214	214	100.0	266	24.3
Manganese Bronze	13	101	83	82.2	59	(28.9)
Metalrax	14	43	45	104.7	82	80.0
W.E.Norton	9	39	37	94.8	29	(21.6)
TACE	9 ½	51	29	56.9	31	6.9
Vickers	144	242	182	75.2	210	15.4
				Average gain for sector		37.8%
Food						
Barker & Dobson	3 ½	15	13 ¾	91.7	20	45.5
George Bassett	68	157	143	91.1	113	(21.0)
Hillards	89	300	195	65	300	53.8
Robertson	75	150	138	92	151	9.4
				Average gain for sector		21.9%
Hotels						
Grand Met	62	109	113	103.7	179	58.4
Ladbroke	89	215	201	93.5	220	9.4
Prince of Wales *	13	40	53	137.5	112	111.3
				Average gain for sector		59.7%

Table 6.4. *(cont'd)*

Share	1977/78 low	1977/78 high	Price at 5 May 78	% of 77/78 high	Price at 4 May 79	% gain (loss)
Industrials						
Associated Sprayers	14	35	33	94.3	68	106.0
Bath & Portland	28½	103	103	65.0	57	(14.9)
Beecham	372	693	664	95.8	725	9.2
Boots	115	244	219	89.8	235	7.3
Carlton Industries	57	175	185	105.7	275	48.6
Celestion	11½	37	35	94.6	35½	1.4
Centreway	54	210	242	115.2	360	48.8
Change Wares	5	35	24½	70.0	18	(26.5)
Cope Allman	37	65½	60½	92.4	80	32.2
Diploma	56	180	154	85.6	334	116.8
Dobson Park	37	79	83	105.1	117	41.0
Dundonian	24	64½	50	77.5	47	(6.0)
Duple	5¾	14	14	100	27½	96.0
Eastern Produce	21	95	95	100	83	12.6
Elliott Peterboro	14	44	22	50	26	18.2
Elson & Robbins	37	78	79	101.3	100	26.6
George Ewer	15	27	28	103.7	41	46.4
Ferguson	37½	105	95	90.5	122	28.4
Fertleman	19	41	29	70.7	28	(3.4)
Gieves Group	30	96	101	105.2	134	32.7
Halma	14	64	60	93.8	68	13.3
Hunting Assoc.	74	218	220	100.9	233	5.9
Johnson Cleaners	27	86	100	116.3	152	52.0
Myson Group	38	74	73 xd	98.6	83 xd	13.7
Neil & Spencer	22	83	102	122.9	188	84.3
Parker Knoll	37	126	106	84.1	107	0.9
Pentland	6	26	21	80.8	34	61.9
Phillips Patents	6	19	15	78.9	23	53.3
Rank	128	276	248	89.9	286	15.3
Redfearn Glass	77	327	275	84.1	260	(5.5)
Reed Executive	15	47	52 xd	110.6	156	200.0
Securicor	46	87	98	112.6	188	91.8
Sketchley	55	109	102	93.6	186	82.3
Stag Furniture	28	114	102	89.5	197	93.1
Talbex	3	24½	23	93.8	13½	(41.3)
Toye	15	49	47	95.9	85	80.9
Turner & Newall	130	252	176	69.8	166 xd	(5.7)

Average gain for sector 37.1%

Share	1977/78 low	1977/78 high	Price at 5 May 78	% of 77/78 high	Price at 4 May 79	% gain (loss)
Leisure						
Boosey & Hawkes	84	212	191	90.1	194 xd	2.1
Campari	25	132	131	99.2	121	(9.0)
Horizon	24	92	106 xd	115.0	260 xd	239.6
Zetters	21	55	55	100.0	74	34.5

Average gain for sector 66.8%

Table 6.4. *(cont'd)*

Share	1977/78 low	high	Price at 5 May 78	% of 77/78 high	Price at 4 May 79	% gain (loss)
Insurance						
Guardian Royal	167	296	234		290 xd	23.9
				Average gain for sector		23.9%
Motors						
Alexanders	4½	22½	18	80.0	18½	2.8
Godfrey Davis	28	87½	86½	98.9	126	45.7
Zenith	58	115	92	80	83	(9.8)
				Average gain for sector		12.9%
Shipping						
Euro Ferries	53½	116	99	85.3	176	77.8
P & O	95	175	119½	68.3	86	(28.0)
				Average gain for sector		24.9%
Textiles						
J.Beales	33	67	55	82.1	67	21.8
Paper						
Inveresk	46	83	66	79.5	49	(25.8)
Oils						
Tricentrol	100	204	178	87.3	244	37.1

* Prices adjusted for splits and scrip issues.
xd = ex dividend

falling, so as to be ready to invest when the market recovers, it seems to be a reasonable assumption that shares which have not declined as much as the market in general, i.e. strong shares should be the ones in the forefront of the market recovery. In order to rank shares on this basis we need some method of quantifying the strength of a share. A way of doing this is to express the price of the share at the time when we have decided the market is definitely recovering as a percentage of its high value reached during the previous peak, i.e. in the present case its 1977/78 high value. Shares which have fallen from their previous peak, as we expect most of them to have done during the general decline will have a price less than 100% of its peak value. On the other hand, some shares may have moved ahead against the trend of the market during the period between when we tabulated the high low values (i.e. during the early part of 1978) and when we are about to invest (i.e. 5th May 1978). These will give prices more than 100% of the previous peak, and can be considered to be the strongest shares as at 5th May. In Table 6.4 the results of this calculation are given under the heading '% of 1977/78 high'. By this means we can see that the strongest share was John Brown, with a price on 5th May 190% of its 1977/78 high (as the high stood in early 1978). The weakest share was Elliott Peterborough, where the price on 5th May (22p) was 50% of its 1977/78 high of 44p.

Since the overall objective of these exercises is to reduce the list of shares on the back pages of the *Financial Times* right down to a handful, say 30, then we can use this relative strength to reduce our list of the 118 most volatile shares. By doing this, we arrive at the 30 shares shown in Table 6.5. The leader, of course, in terms of relative strength at 5th May 1978 was John Brown, whose price as we have said was nearly double its price at its previous peak during

Table 6.5. The 30 strongest shares selected from the list of volatile shares given in Table 6.4. The shares are those which declined least or even advanced from their 1977/78 high values by 5th May 1978

Share	Price on 5 May 78 as % of 1977/78 high	% gain (loss) in year to 4 May 79
John Brown	190.0	81.2
Prince of Wales Hotels	137.5	103.6
Automated Security	133.8	83.5
Neil and Spencer	122.9	84.3
Homecharm	121.3	156.8
Hoveringham	120.3	24.7
Johnson Cleaners	116.3	52.0
Monk	116.3	(30.0)
Centreway	115.2	48.8
Horizon	115.0	239.6
Brooke Tool	114.0	50.0
Shermans	113.6	16.0
Securicor	112.6	91.8
Forminster	112.4	64.7
Maple	111.8	63.0
Reed Executive	110.6	200.0
United Scientific	109.9	(17.7)
Electrocomponents	109.0	123.6
Time Products	106.3	83.0
Comet Radiovision	106.1	32.6
Carlton Industries	105.7	48.6
Gieves Group	105.2	32.7
Dobson Park	105.1	41.0
Metalrax	104.7	80.0
Rosgill	103.7	121.4
Grand Metropolitan	103.7	58.4
George Ewer	103.7	46.4
MFI	102.6	38.7
Elson and Robbins	101.3	46.4
Duple	100.0	96.0
	Average gain for the group 70.2%	

1977/78. The last of the 30 is Duple, which had just reached its previous high value once again.

In order that we can justify the assertion that strength is a good criterion for selecting shares, we have to show that this group of 30 performed better than the 118 from which they were chosen. Table 6.5 lists the gains (or losses) which these shares made in the year from 5th May 1978 and we can see that the average gain for the 30 was 70.2%. This has to be compared with the 48.4% gain which the 118 shares averaged for the year, which shows us that picking shares on the basis of their recent strength was successful in improving our profit for the year. Only two of the shares in the list, Monk and United Scientific were standing lower at the end of the year. Thus, in selecting a small number, say four to six shares, from this list for actual investment, there is only a small chance that one of these two losing shares would have been included.

On the question of the strength of shares, of course, one could take an opposite point of view to that put forward here. One might say that rather than select shares which have not declined very much during the fall of the market, we should select those shares which have fallen the furthest, since they have the greatest potential for profit when they recover. However, one has to ask why these shares have fallen further than the market. If there is no obvious reason, in terms of the company's profits, the loss of a large contract, some calamity at the factory, or political news which affects the company's prospects etc., then perhaps the shares are oversold, and they may well undergo a dramatic reversal of the downward trend when the rest of the market recovers. What if, however, there is something fundamentally wrong with the company's prospects, or at least investors think there is something wrong? In that case, the trouble may not sort itself out, or be thought to be sorting itself out, in time for the market recovery, and the shares may then continue their downward drift.

It is relatively easy to check on this contrary point of view by tabulating the gains or losses during the year for those thirty companies which had declined the *most* during the market fall. These results are listed in Table 6.6 with the 'weakest' share being that of Elliot Peterborough, standing at 50% of the previous high, and the 30th share being Redfearn Glass, standing at 84.1%. The overall gain in value of these shares at the end of the year was only 15.7%, which is much worse than the gain in the All Share Index, and very much worse than the performance of the 30 'strongest' shares, which showed a gain of 70.2% for the year. In addition to that, 12 of the 30 shares showed a loss for the period, and therefore the chance is very high that in a portfolio of say four or five shares, several of these losing shares would have been included.

Having reduced the thousands of shares in which it is possible to invest right down to the list of 30 shown in Table 6.5, we are not suggesting that the gain shown in Table 6.5 would have been made in practice. This is because we are not discussing selling in this chapter. The following chapter on selling of shares will show that it is unlikely that any of the shares, shown in Table 6.5, if bought on 5th May 1978 would still be held a year later. Because of the 'fail-safe'

Table 6.6. The 30 weakest shares selected from the list of volatile shares given in Table 6.4. The shares are those which declined the most from their 1977/78 high values by 5th May 1978

Share	Price on 5 May 78 as % of 1977/78 high	% gain (loss) in year to 4 May 78
Elliot Peterborough	50.0	18.2
EMI	56.7	(20.8)
TACE	56.9	(6.9)
Ratners	60.7	36.8
Hillards	65.0	53.8
Bath & Portland	65.0	(14.9)
Inveresk	66.0	(25.8)
P & O	68.3	(28.0)
Turner & Newall	69.3	(5.7)
Change Wares	70.0	(26.5)
Fertleman	70.7	(3.4)
Vickers	75.2	15.4
Energy Services	77.2	175.0
Dundonian	77.5	(6.0)
Phillips Patents	78.9	53.3
Alexanders	80.0	2.8
Zenith	80.0	(9.8)
Pentland	80.8	61.9
Newarthill	80.8	40.0
Phoenix	80.8	(4.4)
London Brick	81.4	2.9
Comben	81.5	29.0
J.Beales	82.1	21.8
Manganese Bronze	82.2	(28.9)
Cableform	83.5	16.7
J.Walker	83.5	53.5
Plessey	83.8	8.2
Babcock & Wilcox	83.8	54.7
Parker Knoll	84.1	0.9
Redfearn	84.1	(5.5)
	Average gain for the group 15.7%	

mechanism built into the selling rules, the two losing shares Monk and United Scientific would actually have been sold at a profit because their price did move upwards from May 1978 onwards. It just happened that when they retreated from their peak, they fell lower than their prices on 5th May 1978. The whole theme of this chapter is simply to develop a method of selecting shares such that they outperform the rest of the market over whichever time period we feel is suitable to make the comparison. The time period has to be sufficiently long for the consistent nature of the improved performance to become obvious. Thus a 1-year period would appear to be satisfactory from this point of view, and

Table 6.7. Price movement of the shares of the FT 30 constituent companies during the year 9 March 79 to 8 March 80

Share	Price at 9 March 79	Price at 8 March 80	% gain (loss)
Allied Breweries	95	74	(22.1)
Beecham	708	125	(29.0)
Blue Circle	295	310	5.1
BOC	76	65	(14.5)
Boots	220	192	(12.8)
Bowater	202	173	(14.3)
BP	1116	386	38.4
J. Brown	99	55	(44.4)
Cadbury Schweppes	58	61 ½	6.0
Courtaulds	115	70	(39.1)
Distillers	249	205	(17.7)
Dunlop	66	65	(1.5)
EMI	122	123	0.8
GEC	385	377	(2.1)
Glaxo	557	248	(11.0)
Grand Metropolitan	143 xd	132	(7.7)

showed convincingly that the two properties of high volatility and high relative strength at the moment a buying signal is given by the FT Index lead to a vastly improved capital gain compared with a random selection of shares.

Of course it would be reckless to base an investment philosophy solely on an analysis of share price movements for 1 year. We have to adopt the same attitude to the selection of shares as we did for determining buying profits. In the latter case we put forward the 13-week moving average because it had constantly been right in signalling substantial moves upward in the market for a considerable number of years. In the case of share selection, the procedure we have just worked through has also been consistently successful for a number of years in picking the winners. Since the most recent time period is the more relevant, and has the greatest impact, we can examine how the selection procedure has worked for 1979/80, taking the buying signal of the 9th March 1979 (see last chapter) as the starting point. Another interesting aspect is that in this 12-month period, the FT Index actually fell from 515.4 on 9th March 1979 to 455.7 on 8th March 1980, a fall of 11.6%, so this is a very good test of our method, since the best outcome from our point of view would be to end up with a list of 30 shares which actually gained in value while the rest of the market fell.

The price movements of the shares of the FT 30 constituent companies are shown in Table 6.7. Of these 30, 24 shares fell during the 12-month period and only six rose in value. The best performer was P & O, whose shares rose by 40.5% during the period, and the worst performer was John Brown, whose shares fell by 44.4%. The average loss for the group of 30 was 10.1%. Once again, these companies did worse than the rest of the market, since the All Share

Share	Price at 9 March 79	Price at 8 March 80	% gain (loss)
GKN	273	266	(2.6)
Hawker Siddeley	240	176	(26.7)
ICI	404 xd	388	(4.0)
Imperial	103	75	(27.2)
London Brick	75 ½	75	(0.7)
Lucas	295	239	(19.0)
Marks & Spencer	103	93	(9.7)
P & O	74	114	40.5
Plessey	111	145	30.6
Tate & Lyle	144	142	(1.4)
Tube Investments	388	292	(24.7)
Turner & Newall	166	122	(26.5)
UDS	106	70	(33.9)
Vickers	185	128	(30.8)
		Average loss for the group 10.1%	

* shares split.
FT Index fell from 515.4 to 455.7 for a loss of 11.6%.
All Share Index rose from 256.23 to 256.78 for a gain of 2.15%.

Index rose from 256.23 to 256.78, for a small gain of 2.15%. Since previously we decided that the best measurement of the market is obtained by using the All Share Index, we shall do the same again and measure our shares against this gain of 2.15% during the period.

The most volatile shares, on the basis of the ratio of the high to low values for 1978/79 were chosen on 13th January 1979. These shares, 166 in all, are listed in Table 6.8. Their prices at 9th March 1979, when the buying signal was given, are expressed as a percentage of the previous high value, so giving as before a means of deciding on the share strength. Also given in Table 6.8 are the prices on 9th March 1979 and on 8th March 1980, 1 year later, and the gain or loss during that period. The average gain in the total number of 166 shares was 1.4%, so that once again choosing shares on the basis of volatility is successful in yielding shares with a performance superior to that of the market as measured by the FT Index, and fairly similar to the market as measured by the All Share Index.

As far as strength is concerned, the top 30 of these volatile shares are listed in Table 6.9. The best performer was Gripperrods (100% gain), and the worst performer Boardman (69.6% loss). The average gain for the group was 4.6%, so that these 30 shares performed about three times as well as the group of 166 shares from which they were selected. Thus, once again, selection of shares on

Table 6.8. Shares chosen in early 1979 on the basis of volatility

Share	1978/79 Low	1978/79 High	Price at 9 March 79	% of 78/79 high	Price at 8 March 80	% gain (loss)
Breweries						
Arthur Bell	140	211	198	93.8	178	(10.1)
L.Gordon	18	29	26	89.7	52	100.0
Invergordon	83	164	190	115.8	219	15.2
Irish Distillers*	54 ½	98 ½	109	110.6	77	(29.4)
				Average gain for sector 18.9%		
Building						
Benlox	15	31	27	87.0	25 ½	(5.5)
Brit.Dredging	21	41	34	82.9	26	(23.5)
Brown & Jackson*	4 ¾	56	70 ¼	125.7	175	149.1
C.Robey 'A'	22	43	40	93.0	32 ½	(18.8)
Costain	122	223	178	79.8	152	(14.6)
Fed.Land	34	56	67	119.6	62	(7.5)
Francis Parker	11 ½	21	21	100.0	19	(9.5)
Helical Bar	21	41	29	70.7	29 xd	0
Hewden Stuart	41	74 ½	74	99.3	63	(14.8)
Wm Heywood	64	157 ½	88	55.8	82	(6.8)
Howard Shut	12 ½	22 ¼	23	103.4	22	(4.3)
Edward Jones	10	17	14	82.4	14	0
Milbury	30 ¾	69	66	95.6	52	(21.2)
S.Miller	9	18	13	72.2	10	(23.1)
Pochins	82	172	125	72.7	156	24.8
Streeters	20	38	33	86.8	22	(33.3)
Vectis Stone	12	23	30	130.4	31	3.3
Westbrick Products	30	66	70	106.1	57	(18.6)
Wettern Bros	56	116	80	69.0	93	16.3
Wiggins Con.	22	37	34 xd	91.9	31	(8.8)
Wimpey	63	101	86	85.1	78	(9.3)
				Average gain for sector − 1.2%		
Chemicals						
British Benzole	19	36 ½	44	120.5	47	6.8
Burrell	8 ¾	14 ¾	12	81.4	7 ¼	(39.6)
J. Halstead	13 ¾	30	36	120.0	46 ½	29.2
Stewart Plastics	54	95	93	97.9	74	(20.4)
Wardle	17 ½	36 ½	33 ½ xd	91.8	30 xd	(8.9)
				Average gain for sector − 6.6%		
Stores						
Bambers*	10 ½	60	90	150.0	91	1.1
Blackman	13	25 ½	18 ½	72.5	9 ½	(48.6)
Boardman	12	23	28	121.7	8 ½	(69.6)
Burton Group	52 ½	100	91	91.0	123	35.2
S.Casket	13	42	41	97.6	31	(24.4)
Cope Sportswear	28	57	50	87.7	27	(46.0)

Table 6.8. *(cont'd)*

Share	1978/79 Low	1978/79 High	Price at 9 March 79	% of 78/79 high	Price at 8 March 80	% gain (loss)
Dewhirst	33¾	67½	83¼	123.5	69	(17.1)
Ellis & Goldstone	17	31	27	87.1	21	(22.2)
Foster Bros.*	40½	92½	107	115.7	90	(15.8)
Gratton Ware	89	150	100	66.7	82	(28.0)
Greenfields	31	53½	60	112.1	50	(16.7)
K.Henderson	42	91	94	103.3	212	125.5
Homecharm*	33¼	86¾	114	131.5	139	21.9
Lee Cooper*	51	121¼	173¼	142.9	290	67.4
MFI*	18	62½	125	200.0	87	(30.4)
Maple & Co.	13	25	22½	90.0	29½	31.1
Owen Owen	68	128	122	95.3	111	(9.0)
Raybeck	52	102	112	109.8	71	(36.6)
Rosgill	11	36	32 xd	88.9	24	(25.0)
S & U Stores	9	23½	20	85.1	15	(25.0)
H.Samuel	118½	204	197	96.7	149	(24.4)
A.G.Stanley*	24¼	64	75.7	118.2	81	7.3
Status Discount*	20¼	35½	58¼	164.3	66	13.3
Steinberg Group	13	23	22	95.7	18	18.2
Time Products*	33¾	70¾	71¾	101.4	66	(8.0)
Jas.Walker	64	133	134	100.8	96	(28.4)
Waring & Gillow	67¼	131	142	108.4	118	(16.9)
Wearwell	12¾	40½	30	74.1	49½	(65.0)

Average gain for sector − 3.8%

Electrical

Share	Low	High	9 March 79	% of 78/79 high	8 March 80	% gain (loss)
A.B.Electronic	85	166	208	125.0	156	(25.0)
Audiotronics	15	37	19	51.3	7	(63.2)
Cray Electronics	17	41	42	102.4	37 xd	(11.9)
Derritron	14½	26	26	100.0	23	(11.5)
Dreamland	19	39	42	107.7	61	45.2
Dubilier	14½	29	33	113.8	41	24.2
Electrocomponents	159	335	412	123.0	525	27.4
Energy Services	10½	20½	25¾	125.6	26½	2.9
Highland Electronics	21	59	60	101.7	57	(5.0)
Kode International	77	153	226	147.7	205	(9.3)
MK Electric	137	243	228	93.8	174	(23.7)
Wholesale Fittings	122	240	300	125.0	580	93.3
H.Wigfall	146	276	270	97.8	250	(7.4)

Average gain for sector 2.8%

Engineering

Share	Low	High	9 March 79	% of 78/79 high	8 March 80	% gain (loss)
Anderson S'clyde	38	71	72	101.4	71	(1.4)
Barton & Sons	38	73	75	102.7	49	(34.6)
Birmingham Mint	58	138	141	102.2	184	30.5
John Brown	45	99½	99	99.4	55	(44.4)
Bullough	100	175	242	138.2	166	(31.4)

Table 6.8. *(cont'd)*

Share	1978/79 Low	1978/79 High	Price at 9 March 79	% of 78/79 high	Price at 8 March 80	% gain (loss)
Burgess Prods	30	63	66	104.8	60	(9.0)
Delson & Co.	18	34	27	79.4	53	(96.3)
Drake & Scull	15 ½	38	45	118.4	44 xd	(2.2)
G.M.Firth	20	40	37	92.5	30	(18.9)
Hampson Inds.	8⅝	19	14 ½	76.3	11	(24.0)
Manganese Bronze	54	101	58	57.4	31	(46.6)
Meggitt Holdings	11 ½	24	32	133.3	23 xd	(28.1)
Metalrax*	25	45	58 ¼	129.6	60	3.0
Mining Supplies	27	62	81 ½	131.4	89	9.2
W.E.Norton	13¾	35	32 ½	92.8	14	(56.9)
G.Saville	17 ½	35	43 ¼	124.3	38	(12.1)
Startrite	32	73 ½	77	105.4	48	(38.1)
United Engineering	26	87	112	128.7	115	2.6
Victor Products	41	138	143	103.6	160	11.9
Wheway Watson	12 ½	24	21	87.5	15	(28.6)
Wombwell Foundry	18	42	36 ½	86.9	25	(31.5)

Average gain of sector − 12.1%

Food

Share	1978/79 Low	1978/79 High	Price at 9 March 79	% of 78/79 high	Price at 8 March 80	% gain (loss)
Assoc.Fisheries	38	71	42	59.2	61	45.2
Avana Group	28 ½	85	100	117.6	117 xd	17.0
Batleys of York	48	98	100	102.0	110	10.0
Cullens Stores	73	153	136	88.9	146	7.4
L.C.Edwards	8 ½	34	35	102.9	56	60.0
G.F.Lovell	20	60	62	103.3	78 xd	25.8
Morgan Edwards	22	82	87	106.1	123	41.3
Pyke Holdings	30	73	57	78.1	53	(7.0)

Average gain of sector 25.0%

Hotels

Share	1978/79 Low	1978/79 High	Price at 9 March 79	% of 78/79 high	Price at 8 March 80	% gain (loss)
Brent Walker	35	68	61	89.7	73	19.6
Prince of Wales	25 ½	98	125	127.6	73	(41.6)
Warner Hols	22	40	43	107.5	45	4.7

Average gain of sector − 5.8%

Industrial

Share	1978/79 Low	1978/79 High	Price at 9 March 79	% of 78/79 high	Price at 8 March 80	% gain (loss)
Alpine Holdings	36	82	94	114.6	120	27.7
A.Arenson	17	45	60	133.3	50	(16.6)
Assoc.Sprayers	37	60	66	110.0	64	(3.0)
Barrow Hepburn	27	52	31	59.6	35	12.9
Bellair Cosmetics	12 ½	27	24	88.9	19	(20.8)
Black Arrow	26	46	39	84.8	24	(38.5)
Burns Anderson	16	30 ¼	24 ½	81.0	44	79.6
Change Wares	12 ½	26 ½	16 ½	62.2	8 ½	(48.5)
Christies Intl	70	161	142	88.2	170	19.7
Cosalt	40 ½	82	56	68.3	41	(26.8)

Table 6.8. *(cont'd)*

Share	1978/79 Low	1978/79 High	Price at 9 March 79	% of 78/79 high	Price at 8 March 80	% gain (loss)
Crosby Spring	5½	19	18	94.7	20	11.1
De La Rue	230	500	433	86.6	625	44.3
Diamond Styli	10½	19	17	89.5	17	0
Dobson Park	67	122	117	95.9	108	(7.7)
Dundonian	28	57	52	91.2	52	0
Duple Intl.	12	24	24	100.0	25	4.2
Durapipe*	46½	80	62½	78.1	43	(31.2)
E.C.Cases	9½	18	15	83.3	13	(13.3)
G.Ewer	20½	38¼	43	112.4	52½	22.1
E.Fogarty	26½	98	100½	102.6	77	(23.4)
G.R.(Holdings)	65	132	135	102.3	185	37.0
Gripperrods	37	73	94	128.8	188	100.0
Halma	20½	45½	53	116.5	64	20.8
Hawtin	7¾	14	19¼	137.5	13¾	(28.6)
N.Hay	34	78	65	83.3	54	(16.9)
Hunting Assoc.	90	218	195	89.4	370	(89.7)
I.& J.Hyman	11⅜	28½	31½	110.5	21½	(31.7)
ICL	51½	122	124	101.6	132	6.5
M.James Inds.	9½	17	16¾	98.5	15	(10.4)
Jardine Mathieson	149	307	172	56.0	147	(14.5)
McCleery L'Am	10	19	16	84.2	12	(25.0)
Marling Ind.	17	45	49½	110.0	26½	6.0
Mettoy	36	77	66	85.7	35	(46.9)
Monument	5	11½	7	60.8	3½	(50.0)
J.F.Nash	12	80	80	100.0	67	(16.3)
Phillips Patents	14	26	28	107.7	15	(46.4)
Wm.Press	17	32	26½	82.8	30	13.2
Restmor	38	81	80½	99.4	92	14.2
L.Ryan	8½	17	16½	97.1	12	(27.3)
Scot.Heritable	23	47	53	112.8	44	(17.0)
Sutcliffe Speak.	33¼	72	39	54.2	35	(10.2)
Utd.Guarantee	14½	30	29	96.7	24½	(15.5)
Wood & Sons	19	57	42	73.6	27	(35.7)
				Average gain of sector		− 2.0%
Leisure						
Assoc.Leisure	44½	76½	87	113.7	96	10.3
Barr & WAT	40	119	138	116.0	129	(6.5)
Norton & Wright	79	163	145	89.0	90	(37.9)
Saga Holidays	115	198	236	119.2	195	(17.4)
				Average gain for sector		− 12.9%
Insurance						
Edin.& Gen.Inv.	16½	32	36	112.5	32	11.1
				Average gain of sector		11.1%

Table 6.8. *(cont'd)*

Share	1978/79 Low	1978/79 High	Price at 9 March 79	% of 78/79 high	Price at 8 March 80	% gain (loss)
Motors						
Hanger Inv.	21	51	46	90.1	53	15.2
David Nelson	5¾	11½	13½	117.4	13	(3.7)
Rolls-Royce Mtrs.	63½	120½	98	81.3	63	(35.7)
				Average gain of sector		−8.1%
Shipping						
Furness Withy	206	348	244	70.1	370	51.6
Mersey Dock Unit	12½	39¾	34	85.5	19½	(42.6)
W.Runciman	57	115	71	61.7	107	50.7
				Average gain of sector		19.9%
Textiles						
Brit.Enkalon	10	20	19	95.0	11½	(39.5)
Dawson Intl	49½	105	111	105.7	96	(13.7)
Nova (Jersey)	24	50	37	74.0	51	37.8
Small & Tidmas	20	46	50	108.7	75	50.0
				Average gain of sector		8.7%
Papers						
Ault & Wiborg	29	46	46	100.0	49	6.5
Saatchi*	22	48½	57	116.0	160	180.7
Woodrow Wyatt	11	21	20	95.2	22	10.0
				Average gain of sector		65.7%
Oils						
Burmah	42	93	96	103.2	225	134.4
Ultramar	182	284	282	99.3	502	78.0
				Average gain of sector		106.2%

* Adjusted for share splits and scrip issues.
Average gain for whole list = 1.4%

the basis of high volatility and strength results in a far superior performance to the market in general.

The poorer performance of the whole market during this 6-month period is reflected in the fact that a much larger number of shares, 13 in all, made a loss over the 6 months. However, a point to bear in mind is that we would not have been riding these shares downwards but would have sold them only just off their peak values, as shown in the next chapter.

Table 6.9. The 30 strongest shares selected from the volatile shares listed in Table 6.8. The shares are those which had advanced most from their 1978/79 high values by 9 March 1979

Share	Price on 9 March 79 as % of 1978/79 high	% gain (loss) in year to 8 March 80
MFI	200.0	(30.4)
Status Discount	164.3	13.3
Bambers	150.0	1.1
Kode International	147.7	(9.3)
Lee Cooper	142.9	67.4
Bullough	138.3	(31.4)
Hawtin	137.5	(28.6)
Caplan Profile*	134.9	
A.Arenson	133.3	(16.6)
Meggitt	133.3	(28.1)
Homecharm	131.5	21.9
Mining Supplies	131.4	9.2
Vectis Stone	130.4	3.3
Metalrax	129.6	3.0
Gripperrods	128.8	100.0
Utd Engineering	128.7	2.6
Prince of Wales Htls	127.6	(41.6)
Brown and Jackson	125.7	149.1
Energy Services	125.6	2.9
AB Electronic	125.0	(25.0)
Wholesale Fittings	125.0	93.3
G.Saville	124.3	(12.1)
Dewhirst	123.5	(17.1)
Electrocomponents	123.0	(27.4)
Bentima*	122.4	
Boardman	121.7	(69.6)
British Benzole	120.5	6.8
J.Halstead	120.0	29.2
Fed.Land	119.6	(7.5)
Saga Holidays	119.2	(17.4)
	Average gain for group	4.6%

* Share no longer quoted.

The 30 weakest shares in the list of volatile shares are listed in Table 6.10. These range from Wilson Walton, which stood at only 39.5% of its 1978/79 high by 9th March 1979, down to Burns Anderson, which was at 81% of its 1978/79 high on that date. The average gain for the whole group over the 6-month period was 2.5%, which is of course somewhat better than the 1.4% gain of the whole group of volatile shares.

Table 6.10. The 30 weakest shares selected from the list of volatile shares listed in Table 6.8. The shares are those which declined the most from their 1978/79 high values by 9 March 79

Share	Price on 9 March 79 as % of 1978/79 high	% gain (loss) in year to 8 March 80
Wilson Walton*	39.5	
FPA Construction*	50.0	
Audiotronics*	51.3	
Sutcliffe Spkman	54.2	(10.2)
Wm Heywood	55.8	(6.8)
Jardine Mathieson	56.0	(14.5)
Manganese Bronze	57.4	(46.0)
Assoc.Fisheries	59.2	45.2
Barrow Hepburn	59.6	12.9
Monument	60.8	(50.0)
W.Runciman	61.7	50.7
Change Wares	62.2	(48.5)
Gratton	66.7	(28.0)
Cosalt	68.3	(26.8)
Clifford & Snell*	68.4	
Wettern Bros.	69.0	16.3
Furness Withy	70.1	51.6
Helical Bar	70.7	0
S.Miller	72.2	(23.1)
Blackman	72.5	(48.6)
Pochins	72.7	24.8
Wood & Sons	73.6	(35.7)
Nova (Jersey)	74.0	37.8
Wearwell	74.1	65.0
Hampson	76.3	(24.0)
Durapipe	78.1	(31.2)
Pyke	78.1	(7.0)
Delson	79.4	96.3
Costain	79.8	(14.6)
Burns Anderson	81.0	79.6
	Average gain for group	2.5%

* Share no longer quoted.

Chapter 7

When to Sell

Correct selling is a much more difficult aspect of stock market investment than correct buying. The main reason for this is the greater number of psychological barriers which have to be overcome before carrying out a selling decision. In buying, usually the only problem is one of overcoming one's impatience to get invested, when frequently the wisest course is to wait a little longer until the appropriate signals appear to show that the investment climate has turned favourable. In selling, the problems nearly all stem from the fact that you feel that you own a piece of the company and so form a kind of attachment to the shares of that company. It is much easier to do nothing than to take a positive decision to sell; selling appears to be an admission of failure, while holding on offers the prospect of being proved right in having bought the particular company's shares in the first place, if it recovers from what you are absolutely convinced is a temporary setback. A characteristic of nearly all amateur investors is an inability to accept that a share has passed its peak and to presume that the present hiccup in its upward trend is only one more of a number of temporary setbacks which it has suffered during its rise. After all, how are we to distinguish the present retreat from all the previous minor ones? By constantly convincing oneself that the turning point is just around the corner all the profit which accumulated from the correct decision to buy can be allowed to trickle, or even flood, away.

The reasonable way around this problem is twofold. Firstly, we must only treat company shares as pieces of paper, and form no other relationship with them other than that they are a means of making a profit. Secondly, we must have a rigid set of rules that tell us when to sell, and that must be obeyed instantly, without any ifs or buts. If sometimes they fail, that has to be accepted, but does not mean that we abandon the rules unless we can find better ones to put in their place. If our set of rules has worked reasonably well in the past at getting us out of a losing situation, we can reasonably expect them to do the same for us in the future. They will not work all the time, because nothing in the stock market can be predicted with absolute certainty, but if they work four times out of five, we are bound to come out ahead in the long term, and that would be most unlikely if we based our selling decision upon personal feelings or instinct.

Our set of rules must err on the side of caution, since our overall philosophy is to increase our capital when market conditions are favourable, and preserve it from loss when conditions are unfavourable. It is far preferable to have sold and then see the shares continue on their upward path, than not to sell and then see them slide even further. If we have sold prematurely, we still have the option of repurchasing the same share, or of finding another one which we hope will rise, or even of depositing the money in a building society until the next change in market conditions. If we do end up buying the same shares again a few weeks later, we should look upon the commission we have paid on the 'round trip' as an insurance premium which we paid to protect our capital and reflect that that happened to be the one case in five that the rules got us out too soon.

There are three useful methods that we can use to indicate when we should sell a particular holding. Two of these, which you will probably be most comfortable with until you gain experience, give unambiguous signals to sell, based simply upon numerical values which you have calculated. The third depends upon drawing trend lines (a fuller discussion appears in Chapter 8) and, therefore, is rather more subjective but with experience can be far superior to the numerical methods.

The first numerical method is based upon a 13-week moving average of the share price, while the second sets a floor which is the lowest price attained in the previous 9 months. A turndown of the average or a downwards penetration of the floor is the signal to sell.

THIRTEEN-WEEK MOVING AVERAGE

The method of calculating a moving average has been discussed already in Chapter 3. As pointed out there, a moving average gives us a line which is much smoother than the plot of the data from which it is derived. The gain in smoothness has to be paid for somehow, and this payment is the fact that the moving average is lagging in time behind the present. The value for a moving average always has to be plotted in the middle of the time span chosen, so that it is lagging behind by one-half of a time span. Thus, for a 13-week moving average, the value which has been computed from the last 13 weeks closing prices must be plotted for the point 7 weeks back. Since our selling signal is based upon a turn down in the moving average, then if we are computing this every week, this time lag makes no difference. As soon as this week's calculated value is less than last week's, that is the signal to sell. Where this time lag does make a difference is when we are looking at graphs of the average plotted over a period of time, such as the examples in this chapter. In those cases, where we see on the graph that the average turned down on such and such a date, we must bear in mind that we would not have been aware at that time that it had turned down until 7 weeks after that date. So, the price at which we would have sold would not be the price where it turned down on the chart, but the price exactly 7 weeks later.

To come back to the present, assuming a situation where we calculate each week the average for the last 13 weeks, then normally we would find that the share price has been falling for a few weeks before the average itself starts to fall. This few weeks of fall is the penalty we have to pay for a greater degree of certainty that the upward trend in the share price has been reversed. Note that we do not mean 'absolute certainty', because nothing is absolutely certain in the stock market. We could increase our degree of certainty about the downturn in the trend of the share price by increasing the span of our moving average, say up to a 51-week moving average. When this turned down we could be even more sure that the rise in the share price was over. But, when you think about it, the delay in that average would be 26 weeks, i.e. 26 weeks would have elapsed before we got a selling signal, by which time of course the share price could have gone down to the basement.

The 13-week moving average is a reasonable compromise between certainty that the share price has started to move down, and receiving a selling signal soon enough to get out before the price has retreated too far from its peak. On past performance in the case of the vast majority of share prices, a turndown in the 13-week moving average has signalled a prolonged fall in the share price lasting for at least a few months. The 13-week moving average has also been fairly successful in not giving selling signals when the dip in the share price is only of a temporary nature, i.e. it does not shake us out of a share unnecessarily. To see how successful this method is, we can look at the weekly closing prices and 13-week moving average for Babcock & Wilcox, which are plotted in Fig. 7.1. Because of the time lag, the moving average terminates 7 weeks before the end of the weekly data. The arrows give the points at which the average can be seen to have started to turn downwards. Table 7.1 shows the share prices

Table 7.1. Selling signals in Babcock & Wilcox, based on the 13-week moving average

Date turndown in average became apparent	Share price (p)	Date share price peaked out	Peak price	% below peak when signalled
16 June 1972	79	28 Apr. 1972	94	15.9
2 Mar. 1973	83	15 Dec. 1972	100	17.0
11 July 1973	94	1 June 1973	98	4.1
14 Sept. 1973	93	17 Aug. 1973	101	7.9
18 July 1975	60	7 June 1975	69	13.0
16 July 1976	84	22 May 1976	89	5.6
4 Nov. 1977	106	9 Sept. 1977	140	24.0
29 Dec. 1978	147	28 Oct. 1978	166	11.4
15 June 1979	155	4 May 1979	198	21.7
				Average 11%

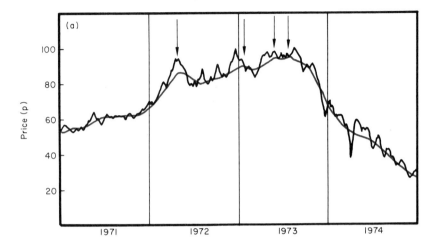

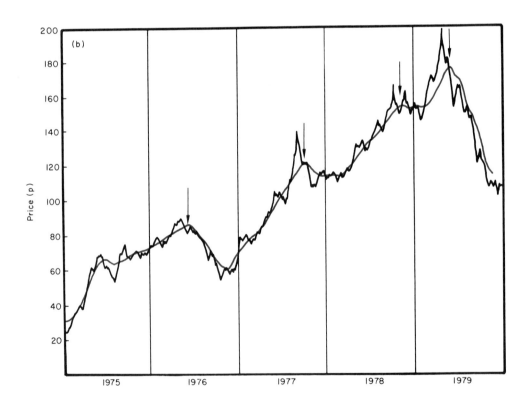

Figure 7.1. Weekly prices of Babcock & Wilcox (black) and the 13-week moving average (red) (a) from 1971 to 1974, (b) from 1975 to 1979. Arrows show the selling signals.

current at the time the average turned down (7 weeks on from the arrows), along with the peak prices attained several weeks before the average gave a 'sell' signal. This then gives us an idea of how much profit has been lost from the peak of the share price, which in turn gives us an indication as to how efficient the signal has been in protecting most of our profit. That the selling signal generated by this method is a very useful one can be judged by the fact that the eight selling signals got us out at an average value of 11% below the peak price at that period in time. There is no way that selling by instinct can maintain that kind of consistency over a number of selling operations and most investors would be quite happy to settle for a method which brings them out within 10 or 11% of the top.

On their own, these selling points do not tell us much about the profit we would have made unless we have also established our buying points. So, although there are four selling signals throughout the period 1972 and 1973, our buying signals, based on the 13-week average of the FT Index would not have allowed us to buy again after the selling signal of 16th June 1972. By following the buying principle outlined in Chapter 5, we would have bought Babcock & Wilcox in early 1971, at a price of about 55p and our selling signal would have got us out in June 1972 at 79p, for a gain of 43.6% over the period. The market next signalled a purchase on 24th January 1975. Babcock shares could then have been bought for 28p. At the selling signal on 18th July we would have obtained 60p for them, a gain of 114.5% The next buying signal was on 19th September 1975, at which time Babcock shares were 77p and we would have sold again on 16th July 1976 at 84p, a gain of 9.1%. The FT 13-week average next indicated a buying situation on 30th December 1976, when Babcocks were 61p and the next selling signal got us out on 4th

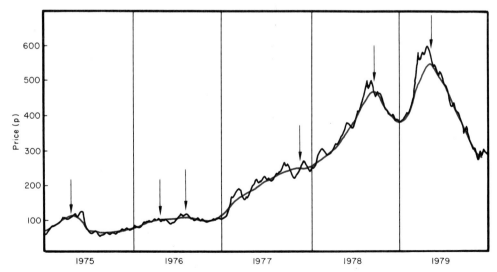

Figure 7.2. Weekly prices of John Brown (black) and the 13-week moving average (red) from 1975 to 1979. Arrows show the selling signals.

Table 7.2. Buying and selling operations in Babcock & Wilcox as signalled by 13-week moving averages (FT Index for buying and share price for selling)

Buying		Selling		
Date	Share price (p)	Date	Share price (p)	% gain (loss)
February 1971	55	16 June 1972	79	43.6
24 Jan. 1975	28	18 July 1975	60	114.3
19 Sept. 1975	77	16 July 1976	84	9.1
30 Dec. 1976	61	4 Nov. 1977	106	73.8
5 May 1978	123	29 Dec. 1978	147	19.5
9 Mar. 1979	169	15 June 1979	155	(8.2)
			Cumulative gain 544%	

November 1977, at 106p for a gain of 73.8%. A buying signal came again on 29th April 1978 when Babcock & Wilcox were 123p and they would have been sold again at the end of December 1978 for 147p, i.e. a gain of 19.5%. The next buying signal came on 9th March 1979, when Babcocks could have been bought for a price of 169p and a selling signal came on 15th June 1979 at a price of 155p for a loss of 8.2%. These buying and selling operations are summarized in Table 7.2.

If the proceeds of selling were reinvested in the next buying operation, the cumulative gain over the five 'round trip' transactions from 1971 to 1978 would have been 544%, so that the capital value would have increased by a factor of about 6 ½ in a period of 8 years.

A vast number of examples could be given here on the operation of the 13-week moving average as a selling signal. However, it is suggested that you carry out such calculations on a share or shares which you have chosen by the method outlined in the last chapter. The data for the shares for a large number of companies for several years back can be obtained from share price charts. The latter can be obtained commercially, as mentioned in Appendix E.

The turndown in the 13-week moving average has been useful in developing selling signals for all shares but is not always as successful in getting us out as near to the peak price as the Babcock & Wilcox case. One example in which this method was less successful is John Brown. A plot of the weekly closing prices and the 13-week average for John Brown shares is shown in Fig. 7.2. Once again, arrows show the points at which selling signals were generated. The dates, 7 weeks after the position of the arrows, at which a turndown in the average became apparent were: 7th June 1975, 28th May 1976, 1st October 1976, 16th December 1977, 4th November 1978 and 15th June 1979. Table 7.3 shows the share prices at the time the signals were given and the dates and prices of the peak values attained by the shares prior to the selling signals. In this case, for the six selling signals, we would have sold at prices averaging 15.5% down from the peak prices at those times. Thus, this is an inferior

Table 7.3. Selling signals in John Brown, based on 13-week moving average

Date turndown in average became apparent	Share price	Date share price peaked out	Peak price	% below peak when signalled
7 June 1975	75	24 May 1975	115	34.8
28 May 1976	82	21 May 1976	90	8.9
1 Oct. 1976	90	14 Aug. 1976	105	14.2
16 Dec. 1977	250	2 Dec. 1977	260	3.8
4 Nov. 1978	415	13 Sept. 1978	490	15.3
15 June 1979	494	4 May 1979	587	15.8
			Average	15.5%

Table 7.4. Buying and selling operations in the shares of John Brown, as signalled by 13-week moving averages

Buying		Selling		
Date	Share price (p)	Date	Share price (p)	% gain
24 Jan. 1975	70	7 June 1975	73	7.1
19 Sept. 1975	52	28 May 1976	82	57.7
30 Dec. 1976	97	16 Dec. 1977	250	157.7
5 May 1978	310	4 Nov. 1978	415	33.9
9 Mar. 1979	478	15 June 1979	494	3.3
		Cumulative gain on five transactions		491%

performance of the selling signals compared with Babcock & Wilcox.

As in the case of Babcock & Wilcox, it is important to look at a complete picture of buying and selling operations. Of the selling signals listed in Table 7.3, the one on 1st October 1976 is superfluous, since the rules we have established for buying would not have allowed us to buy again following the sale on 28th May 1976, until 30th December 1976. During the period in question, it would have been possible to carry out five complete buying and selling operations. These are summarized in Table 7.4. The most successful 'round trip' was the purchase of 30th December 1976 at 97p, which led to a sale on 16th December 1977 at 250p, for a gain of 157.7%. By reinvesting the proceeds of each sale into the next buying operation, a cumulative gain of 491% would have been obtained over the five transactions between 24th January 1975 and 15th June 1979, i.e. over a period of only just over 4 years! By this means you can satisfy yourself that the method works as a means of protecting the greater proportion of the gains which your share has accumulated since the buying signal.

BREAKING THE NINE-WEEK LOW

This method consists of superimposing upon a plot of the share price the lowest level attained in the previous 9 weeks. In the case of a rising share price, this 9-week low moves up from time to time under it. If the share price drops to a point which penetrates this low, this is taken as a signal to sell. There is a similar problem here in choosing the period for which the low operates, i.e. 9 weeks in our case, as there was in the case of a moving average. Too short a low period, such as 3 or 4 weeks could mean that the sale is triggered when the price undergoes only a very temporary setback. Too long a period means that the price has to fall a long way before a selling signal is given. This would mean too large a loss to be acceptable. Because of these factors, calculations on a large number of share prices have shown that a 9-week low is an ideal compromise.

In order to keep a valid comparison with the 13-week moving average method, we shall apply the 9-week low method to the same share prices, Babcock & Wilcox and John Brown. In Fig. 7.3 are plotted the weekly closing prices and the 9 week lows for Babcock & Wilcox for 1971 to 1979. As can be seen from the number of arrows marking the points where the 9-week low was penetrated, this method gives more signals than the moving average: eleven points as opposed to eight. There is no problem of a time lag in the case of violation of the 9-week low, the dates shown on the plot being the dates at which we knew the low was broken and, therefore, is the date at which we would have sold the shares. The selling points were: 2nd June 1972, 2nd March 1973, 14th September 1973, 14th June 1974, 18th July 1975, 4th June 1976, 29th July 1977, 4th November 1977, 24th February 1978, 9th February 1979 and 16th June 1979. The selling points and appropriate share prices for both the 9-week low method and the 13-week moving average method are given in Table 7.5.

Table 7.5. A comparison of the selling points and share prices of the 9-week low and 13-week moving average methods for Babcock & Wilcox 1971 – 1979

9-week low method		13-week average method	
Date	Price	Date	Price
2 June 1972	81	16 June 1972	79
2 Mar. 1973	83	2 Mar. 1973	83
		11 July 1973	94
14 Sept. 1973	93	14 Sept. 1973	93
14 June 1974	46		
18 July 1975	60	18 July 1975	60
4 June 1976	79	16 July 1976	84
29 July 1977	96		
4 Nov. 1977	106	4 Nov. 1977	106
24 Feb. 1978	109		
9 Feb. 1979	143	29 Dec. 1978	147
15 June 1979	155	15 June 1979	155

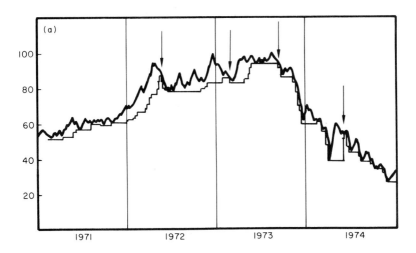

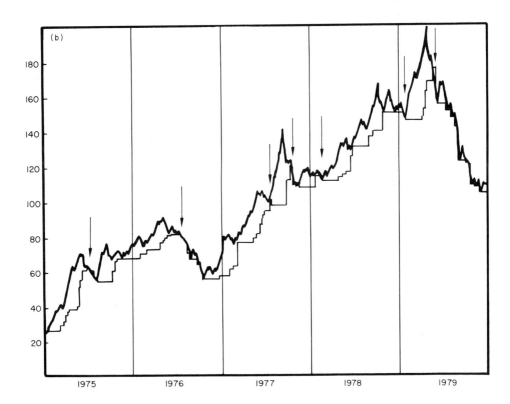

Figure 7.3. Weekly prices of Babcock & Wilcox (heavy line) and the 9-week low (light line) (a) from 1971 to 1974, (b) from 1975 to 1979. Arrows show the selling signals.

The first selling signal, on 2nd June 1972, came 2 weeks before the appropriate moving average signal, enabling us to sell at 81 as opposed to 79. The next three signals are irrelevant because, as shown earlier in Table 7.2, we would not have reinvested until 27th January 1975. The next selling signal on 18th July 1975 was identical for both methods. We would have reinvested again on 19th September 1975 and the next selling signal came on 6th August 1976. This is later by 3 weeks and worse by 7p a share than the signal given by the moving average. We would have reinvested on 30th December 1976 and the 9-week low method would have got us out on 29th July 1977 at 96p, at a period when the moving average gave no signal. Both methods signalled a sale on 4th November 1977 at 106p. We would have bought again on and sold on 9th February 1979 at 143p, according to the 9-week low method. However, by comparison, the moving average method would have told us to sell 2 months earlier, on 29th December 1978 at 147p. We would have bought again on 9th March 1979 and the 9-week low method would have told us to sell on 15th June 1979 at 155p, the same week as the 13-week average signalled.

The final results obtained by either of these methods can be seen, from Table 7.5, to be fairly similar in the case of Babcock & Wilcox shares. As far as John Brown is concerned, more signals were again given by the 9-week low method, as can be seen from the plot of the weekly closing prices and the 9-week low for the period since 1975, in Fig. 7.4. As a comparison with the 13-week average method, the selling points and prices for both the methods for John Brown shares for the period 1975 to 1979 are given in Table 7.6.

There are four signals by the 9-week low method that are superfluous, since our buying methods would not have allowed us to buy again before them. These occurred in 1976, on 17th September and 29th October, since we could

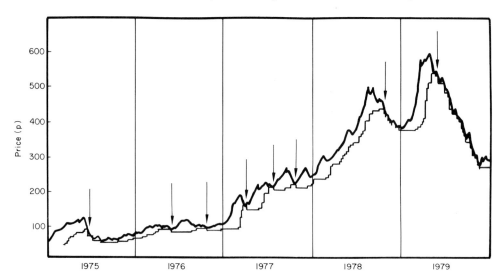

Figure 7.4. Weekly prices of John Brown (heavy line) and the 9-week low (light line) from 1975 to 1979. Arrows show the selling signals.

Table 7.6. A comparison of the selling point and share prices of the 9-week low and 13-week moving average methods for John Brown, 1975 – 1979

| 9-week low method | | 13-week average method | |
Date	Price	Date	Price
7 June 1975	75	7 June 1975	75
4 June 1976	75	28 May 1976	82
8 Apr. 1977	145	1 Oct. 1976	105
28 Oct. 1978	425	16 Dec. 1977	250
25 May 1979	525	4 Nov. 1978	415
		15 June 1979	494

not have bought back after the sale on 4th June 1976 until 20th December 1976 and in 1977 on 29th July and 21st October, since we could not have bought back after the sale on 8th April 1977 until 1978.

On the occasions when the signals were not superfluous, we have one case where the two methods gave a signal on the same date, one occasion where the moving average signalled a sale before the 9-week low method, and two occasions where the 9-week low method got us out slightly before the moving average method, and at a better price. There was also one occasion, 8th April 1977, where the moving average gave no signal.

For a wide range of shares, the 9-week low method signals a selling situation a week or so before the moving average on about three occasions out of five; for the other two the moving average comes first. On the other hand, the 9-week low method also gives us some false signals that cause us to sell prematurely. A premature sale should not cause us to shed any tears for lost profits, however, since we can live to fight another day; probably the best approach to these two methods is to follow both of them, and act on whichever signal comes first. If they both appear at the same time, so much the better. On those occasions when the 9-week low signals first, it is usually possible to gain some confirmation by checking the 13-week average to see if there are any signs of it slowing down in its rate of increase, which it should do a week or so before it actually turns down.

THE RISE – FALL TRENDLINE

When a share price rises over a period of many weeks, a close look at the weekly closing prices during that time usually shows that the price does not rise consistently, week after week, but advances for a few weeks, then slips back perhaps for a week before advancing further. This may happen several times during the course of its rise, so we have a sort of 'two steps forward, one step back' type of situation. The rising price is the result of two things, firstly, the price increases during the weeks the price goes up is greater than the price falls during the weeks it falls, and secondly, the number of weeks for which it advances is greater than the number during which it declines. This is not an invariable fact, but does appear to be true for the majority of occasions. When a share price is falling over a period of many weeks, the opposite will be true — during the period the weekly price falls are greater than the weekly price rises, and the number of weeks for which the price falls is greater than the number of weeks during which the price rises. Idealized versions of both of these situations are shown in Fig. 7.5.

The previous two numerical methods for generating selling signals utilized the changes in the share prices themselves as the basis of the methods, and the number of advancing weeks relative to the number of declining weeks during the overall period of advance of the share price was not of particular importance. The third method for generating selling signals, however, concentrates on this latter aspect and neglects the actual prices themselves. The indicator assumes that a rising price tends to fall into a pattern of x weeks upward and y weeks downward (where x and y are quite small, say 3 or 4 to 1 or 2 respectively), the pattern being repeated several times. It is the break in this pattern which is considered to signal an impending downturn to the actual share price, so therefore tells us to sell.

The indicator itself is extremely easy to plot. At the beginning of the time period we are interested in, we set it at an arbitrary value, such as zero, and each week we increase it by one every time a price is higher than the previous week, and decrease it by one if the price is lower. If the price is unchanged we give the indicator the same value as last week. A weekly record of such an indicator for some mythical share prices is given in Table 7.7.

We can then plot this indicator on the same graph as the share price itself, using the same weeks for the values, but a different vertical scale for the indicator, since it moves only one point (or zero) at a time, whereas the share price of course may move perhaps by 50p a week (Fig. 7.6(a)). The indicator does not itself give us a selling signal. To obtain such a signal, it is necessary to draw a

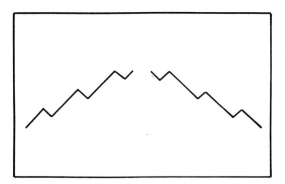

Figure 7.5. Idealized versions of the way in which share prices rise and fall over short periods of time.

7.7. Construction of a weekly rise – fall indicator

Week	Share price	Indicator	Week	Share price	Indicator
1	222	0	10	245	3
2	220	– 1	11	250	4
3	210	– 2	12	260	5
4	215	– 1	13	255	4
5	220	0	14	260	5
6	225	1	15	270	6
7	230	2	16	270	6
8	225	1	17	275	5
9	235	2	18	260	4

(a)

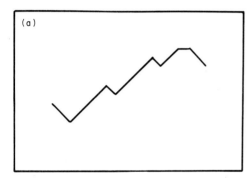

(b)

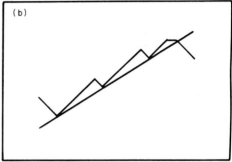

Figure 7.6. (a) The rise – fall indicator plotted for the shares whose prices are given in Table 7.6. (b) A trend line drawn on the rise – fall indicator from (a).

trend line. This is done by joining the bottom points of the saw-tooth shape in Fig. 7.6(a) by a straight line. It will be unlikely that we can join more than two or three such points following a change in direction of the saw-tooth from down to up. Having then established this trend line, our selling signal is given when the indicator, instead of bouncing back up from this line, penetrates it downwards (Fig. 7.6(b)).

Table 7.8. Selling signals for Babcock & Wilcox as given by the penetration of trend lines by the rise – fall indicator

Date	Price	Date	Price
11 May 1972	90	7 Oct. 1977	120
1 June 1973	95	30 Dec. 1978	147
21 June 1975	68	8 June 1979	177
29 May 1976	81		

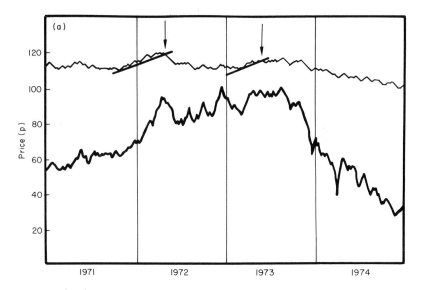

Figure 7.7. Weekly closing prices of Babcock and Wilcox (heavy line) and the rise – fall indicator (light line) (a) from 1971 to 1974, (b) from 1975 to 1979. Selling points are indicated by arrows at the points where the trend lines (short heavy lines) are penetrated by the rise – fall indicator.

Applied to a real case, we can see this indicator, and the weekly closing prices plotted for Babcock & Wilcox shares since 1971, in Fig. 7.7. There are seven trend lines drawn for those situations where the share price is obviously rising: in 1972, 1973, 1975, 1976, 1976/77, 1978 and 1979. For each trend line, the rise – fall indicator approached it several times and bounced back before finally penetrating it. So, when the indicator turns down towards the trend line, we have to watch carefully for that time when it does not bounce back, that being then our selling signal. The dates at which this happened, and the corresponding share prices, are given in Table 7.8.

A comparison of Table 7.8 with Table 7.5 shows that this indicator was superior to both the 13-week moving average method and the 9-week low method. Except for the May 1976 signal, the other signals gave selling indications when the share price was much higher than with the other two methods. Except for 29th December 1978 the signals also came much sooner — several weeks — than the signals from the numerical methods.

The best way of showing the superiority of the rise – fall method over the other two is to calculate the overall gain which would have been achieved by using it in transactions in Babcock & Wilcox, and compare it with the gain of 544% which we showed in Table 7.2 for the 13-week average method, which itself was fairly close to the results obtained by the 9-week low method. This comparison is done in Table 7.9. This time, the gain over the complete set of five transactions, assuming reinvestment of proceeds from sales, is 938%, i.e. the capital value would have been increased by a factor of more than ten during the period.

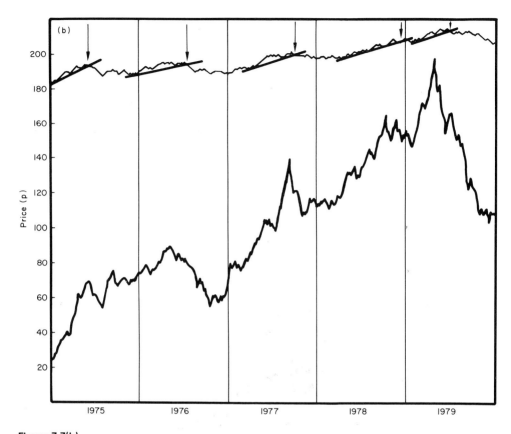

Figure 7.7(b)

Table 7.9. Buying and selling operations in Babcock & Wilcox since 1971, as signalled by the 13-week moving average of the FT Index for buying and the rise – fall indicator for selling

Buying		Selling		
Date	*Price*	*Date*	*Price*	*% gain*
Feb. 1971	55	11 May 1972	90	63.6
24 Jan. 1975	28	21 June 1975	68	142.8
19 Sept. 1975	77	29 May 1976	81	5.2
30 Dec. 1976	61	7 Oct. 1977	120	96.7
9 Mar. 1979	169	30 Dec. 1978	147	19.5
		8 June 1979	177	4.7
			Cumulative gain 938%	

Having shown that this indicator was far superior in giving selling signals for Babcock & Wilcox, it remains to show whether it was superior in the case of John Brown shares, since the chart pattern for this share was rather different from that of Babcock & Wilcox. This indicator and the share prices for John Brown, are shown in Fig. 7.8. In the period from 1975 to 1979 there are five trend lines which were penetrated on 3rd May 1975, 6th February 1976, 5th August 1977, 29th September 1978 and 6th April 1979. The buying and selling operations carried out on John Brown shares, using the 13-week moving average of the FT Index for buying, and the breaking of the trend lines by the rise – fall indicator for selling, are given in Table 7.10.

The cumulative gain on five transactions in John Brown shares, using the rise – fall indicator as a selling indicator, is 578%, i.e. the starting capital would have increased by a factor of nearly seven times by this method over the period since 1975. This is a gain of nearly 90% more than would have been achieved using the 13-week moving average signal for selling.

In these two cases, of Babcock & Wilcox and John Brown shares, the breaking of the trend line of the rise – fall indicator has given a far better signal for selling of the three methods we have discussed. Again this is true for a wide range of shares but there is the slight disadvantage that it takes rather more experience to draw the trend line correctly than is the case with the other methods, which depend upon simple numerical calculation.

It is suggested that you do not plunge immediately into using this trend line signal, but gain experience by applying it to a large number of share prices, obtained from charts as mentioned before. When you are quite happy about

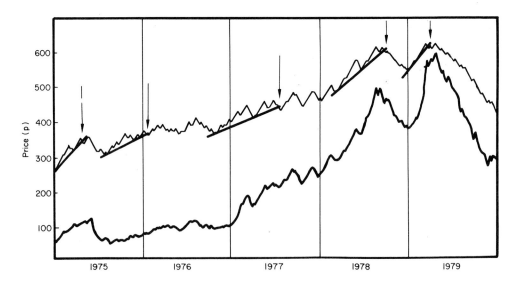

Figure 7.8. Weekly closing prices of John Brown (heavy line) and rise – fall indicator (light line) from 1974 to 1979. Selling points are indicated by arrows at the points where the trend lines are penetrated by the rise – fall indicator.

Table 7.10. Buying and selling operations in John Brown since 1975, as signalled by the 13-week moving average of the FT Index for buying, and the rise – fall indicator for selling

Buying		Selling		
Date	Price	Date	Price	% gain
24 Jan. 1975	70	3 May 1975	95	35.7
19 Sept. 1975	52	6 Feb. 1976	75	44.3
30 Dec. 1976	97	5 Aug. 1977	210	116.5
9 Mar. 1979	478	29 Sept. 1978	435	40.3
		6 Apr. 1979	543	13.6
			Cumulative gain	578%

your ability to use it, you can then consider it to be your major indicator for selling, and use it with confidence. As shown in the above examples, this indicator usually gives its signal some weeks before the moving average or 9-week low methods, and so, when the trend line gives a signal, some slight confirmation should be forthcoming from the other methods in the form of a reduction of the rate at which the 13-week average is climbing and a movement of the share price downwards towards its 9-week low floor.

Although we have shown so far how these selling signals have performed in the case of two shares over a number of years, it might still be argued that the examples are too few to really prove the point about selling signals, and that we need to show many more such examples to be really convincing. In the last chapter we chose a list of 30 shares, on the basis of volatility and relative strength. We showed that during the year following the buying signal in May 1978, our 'top 30' outperformed both the market in general and the Financial Times 30 shares in particular, in terms of percentage gain for the group. In one sense, the selection was perhaps not too meaningful, because we made the assumption that the shares were held for a whole year when we calculated the percentage gain. This ignored any selling signals that might have been generated during the year and gave the results which we showed in Table 6.5. However, if we look at what would have been the real life situation, in which we kept track of the 13-week moving average, the 9-week low, and the rise – fall indicator, then we would have achieved the gains and losses shown in Table 7.11. This table gives, for each of the 'top 30' shares which were listed in Table 6.5, the times the selling signals were given, and the relevant prices. Now we have a much wider basis on which to compare the relative merits of the three different types of selling signal. The table shows that of the 30 shares, the rise – fall indicator gave the best selling price in 20 instances, so that on balance we can say it is the superior indicator. Another point here is that we mentioned earlier that this indicator tended to give its signal before the others, and this is borne out by Table 7.11, because for these 30 shares, in 29 instances the rise – fall indicator signalled before the others, and in the 30th case, it gave its signal at the same time as the 13-week moving average (Grand Metropolitan).

Table 7.11. The selling signals, selling prices and appropriate gains and losses for the 30 strongest shares in Table 6.4 since 5th May 1978

Share	Price at 5 May 78	13-week moving average method			9-week low method			Rise – fall indicator		
		Date	Price	Gain (loss)	Date	Price	Gain (loss)	Date	Price	Gain (loss)
John Brown	324	4 Nov. 78	415	28.1	28 Oct. 78	425	31.2	29 Sept. 78	435	34.3
Prince of W.Htl	53	19 May 79	105	98.1	27 Apr. 79	113	105.5	9 Dec. 78	90	69.8
Automated Sec.	79							6 Apr. 79	133	68.4
Neil & Spencer	102	28 Oct. 78	108	5.9	6 Oct. 78	120	15.0	25 Aug. 78	122	16.4
Homecharm	148							11 Nov. 78	210	41.9
Hoveringham	77	26 Jan. 79	86	11.7	25 Nov. 78	87	13.0	6 Oct. 78	88	14.3
Johnson Clnrs	100	28 Oct. 78	91	(9.0)	28 Oct. 78	91	(9.0)	18 Aug. 78	101	1.0
Monk	100	25 Nov. 78	96	(4.0)	11 Nov. 78	96	(4.0)	4 Nov. 78	98	(2.0)
Centreway	242	28 July 79	333	37.6	29 Sept. 78	257	6.2	8 Sept. 78	278	14.9
Horizon	106							1 Sept. 78	103	(2.8)
Brooke Tool	32	11 Nov. 78	40	25.0	21 Oct. 78	42	23.8	18 Aug. 78	48	50.0
Shermans	12½	15 Sept. 78	13½	8.0	22 Sept. 78	13	4.0	18 Aug. 78	14	12.0
Securicor	98	9 Sept. 78	122	24.5	4 Nov. 78	120	22.4	25 Aug. 78	133	35.7
Forminster	102	11 Nov. 78	102	0	18 Nov. 78	101	(1.0)	25 Aug. 78	104	2.0
Maple	19	4 Nov. 78	20½	7.9	4 Nov. 78	20½	7.9	1 Sept. 78	21½	13.2
Reed Exec.	52	19 June 79	79	51.9	26 Jan. 79	76½	47.1	9 Sept 78	69	32.7
Utd Scientific	322	28 Oct. 78	312	(3.1)	13 Oct. 78	336	4.3	1 Sept. 78	362	12.4
Electrocomps	199	29 Jan. 79	423	112.6	4 Nov. 78	275	38.2	22 Sept. 78	309	55.3
Time Products	136	4 Nov. 78	175	28.6	4 Nov. 78	175	28.6	18 Aug. 78	192	41.2
Comet Radio.	122	28 Oct. 78	136	11.5	28 Oct. 78	136	11.5	1 Sept. 78	149	22.1
Carlton	185	4 Nov. 78	210	13.5	28 Oct. 78	218	17.8	22 Sept. 78	232	25.4
Gieves Group	101	28 Oct. 78	90	(10.9)	28 Oct. 78	90	(10.9)	11 Aug. 78	97	(4.1)
Dobson Park	83	28 Oct. 78	102	22.9	28 Oct. 78	102	22.9	25 Aug. 78	114	37.3
Metalrax	45	11 Nov. 78	48	6.7	4 Nov. 78	48	6.7	29 Sept. 78	52	15.6
Rosgill	14							29 Sept. 78	22	57.1
Grand Met.	113	1 Sept. 78	112	(0.9)	29 Sept. 78	110	(1.8)	1 Sept. 78	112	(0.9)
George Ewer	28	13 Oct. 78	36	28.6	1 Sept. 78	34½	23.2	8 June 78	36½	30.4
MFI	78							1 Sept. 78	131	67.9
Elson & Robbins	79	29 Sept. 78	88	11.4	6 Oct. 78	88	11.4	11 Oct. 78	96	21.5
Duple	14	26 Jan. 79	23½	67.9	22 June 79	24½	75.0	25 Oct. 78	21	50.0

The overall performance of the group is, therefore, best represented by taking the gains and losses which would have resulted in using the rise – fall indicator for selling. By doing this, the overall gain for the 30 shares comes out as 27.8%. At first time this may look extremely disappointing when compared with the 81.8% gain calculated for the top 30 shares had they been held for exactly 1 year. This might even lead us to the conclusion that we could do without a selling indicator altogether and sell our shares 1 year after we buy them! There are, though, two main reasons why the performances in terms of gains and losses, as shown in Table 7.11, when a selling indicator is used, is superior to the gains and losses shown in Table 6.5, when an indicator is not used and we simply hold the shares for a specified time.

1. The *risk* in holding these shares has been greatly reduced. In Table 6.5, it can be seen that two shares lost 30.0 and 17.7% respectively over the 1 year period. With a small portfolio, there is some chance that one or both of these shares are held, together with a few others with small gains, so that the overall portfolio is in a losing situation. From Table 7.11, selling at the times indicated would have resulted in losses in four shares. However, the losses themselves were of 0.9, 2.0, 2.8 and 4.1% respectively, which can almost be considered to be of negligible proportions. Correct selling has therefore reduced the risk of loss for those shares which fail to come up to expectations.
2. Although the overall gain for the 30 shares is less, the gain has been accumulated over a shorter time period than the 1-year period given in Table 6.5. The average period of time for which the 30 shares were held before selling according to the indicators was 19 weeks, i.e. about 4 ½ months. A gain of 27.4% over this period, if compounded to a 1-year period at the same rate of gain is equivalent to an annual gain of more than 90%!

There would have been another chance to reinvest these proceeds within a year of the original purchase, since another buying signal was given by the 13-week moving average of the FT Index on 9th March 1979. As shown in Chapter 6, the new 'top 30' shares for this next investment opportunity only contained three shares that were in our first list: Homecharm, Metalrax and Electrocomponents.

Because of such changes in the shares which have the greatest potential for profit when each new buying opportunity arises, it is essential that a new list be prepared during each market fall. It is not so important to prepare a new list of the 100 or so most volatile shares if two buying opportunities arise within a short time of each other, as has been the case in 1979 but it is still necessary to recalculate the strongest shares for the second occasion, since these will differ substantially from those listed for the first occasion.

Although it is impressive to show that the gain obtained by correct buying and selling of the 30 shares in Table 7.11 would have compounded to an annual gain of about 90%, this does not really tell us how effective these indicators are in getting us out near the peak price. Half of the gain we made may be said to be due to correct buying, while the other half is due to correct selling. A good way to evaluate the selling indicators is to use the methods we applied to the Babcock & Wilcox and John Brown shares, in which we calculated how far down, percentagewise, from the peak price, the indicators told us to sell.

Since we have already decided, based on the information in Table 7.11, that the rise – fall indicator was superior, we need only give the results for that indicator. This is done, for the 30 shares, in Table 7.12. Under the heading '% down from peak price' the smaller the value the better, since of course a figure of 0 would mean that we sold at the exact peak top. Such a figure would not, of course, be obtainable since we never know a peak price was a peak price until after we have passed it and are already on the way down. Ideally, we would like to be told to sell when we were somewhere between 5 and 10% back from the peak — anything less than 5%, consistently, is unrealistic.

Table 7.12. The rise – fall indicator

Share	Peak price (p)	Price when indicator signalled	% down from peak price
John Brown	490	435	11.2
Prince of Wales Hotels	125	90	28.0
Automated Security	145	133	8.3
Neil & Spencer	131	122	6.8
Homecharm	230	210	8.7
Hoveringham	90	88	2.2
Johnson Cleaners	110	101	8.2
Monk	107	98	8.4
Centreway	295	278	6.1
Horizon	121	103	14.8
Brooke Tool	50	48	4.0
Shermans	14 ½	14	3.4
Securicor	135	133	1.5
Forminster	108	104	3.7
Maple	22 ½	21 ½	4.4
Reed Executive	80	69	13.7
United Scientific	379	362	4.5
Electrocomponents	312 ½	309	1.1
Time Products	206	192	6.8
Comet Radiovision	154	149	3.2
Carlton	235	232	1.3
Gieves Group	102	97	4.9
Dobson Park	117	114	2.5
Metalrax	55	52	5.5
Rosgill	31	22	29.0
Grand Metropolitan	119 ½	112	6.3
George Ewer	46	36 ½	20.6
MFI	146	131	10.2
Elson & Robbins	97	96	1.0
Duple	21 ½	21	2.3
			Average 7.8 %

The average 'percentage down from the peak price' for the 30 shares in Table 7.12 is 7.8%, which is an impressive performance. This means that, for an average share which reaches a peak price of 100p before falling back, say to 50p, the indicator would have told us to sell at a price of 92p, and thus would have saved most of the profit we achieved from buying that share in the first place.

The most successful instance for the working of the selling indicator was the case of Elson & Robbins, when we would have got out only 1% down from the peak price — selling at 96p when the peak was 97p. The least successful was Rosgill, where we would have been told to sell 29% down from the peak price. In the table there are six shares in which the rise – fall indicator appeared to be less successful than one would hope. These are John Brown, Prince of Wales Hotels, Horizon, Reed Executive, Rosgill and George Ewer. They bear closer examination because, in fact, the performance of the indicator in these cases is not as bad as would at first appear. In *none* of these instances did the indicator allow profits to dwindle away. What happened was that the indicator got us out too soon and the share price recovered and moved to an even greater high. The percentages in Table 7.12 for these shares are, therefore, unrealistic in the sense that they refer to the *eventual* peak top, which may have occurred months later.

In two cases, Prince of Wales Hotels and Reed Executive, the indicator gave a selling signal on what was a considerable fall in price but was of sufficiently short duration that the 13-week moving average and 9-week low signals were, therefore, not triggered. The latter was triggered some months later. The rise – fall indicator would have got us out within 2.2.% for Prince of Wales Hotels and 5.2% for Reed Executive of the minor peak top, and hence the indicator can be said to have been very effective. As far as George Ewer, Horizon and Rosgill are concerned, the indicator was less satisfactory, shaking us out after what turned out to be a fairly minor drop in the share price. In the case of John Brown, the fall in price was so rapid that we were 11.2% down from the peak top before the indicator was triggered. Even so, the rise – fall indicator was still superior to both the 13-week moving average and the 9-week low method in that particular instance.

If we replace the values for Prince of Wales Hotels and Reed Executive in Table 7.12 by the figures of 2.2 and 5.2%, for the reasons we have just outlined, that we were dealing with a peak on a peak as it were, then the average value of 7.8% for the 30 shares comes down to 6.6.%.

Now we have looked more closely at the working of the rise – fall indicator, we can form a much clearer impression of how it has worked for the 30 shares. For 26 of the shares the indicator worked superbly, getting us out within 6.6% of the peak price attained. For the other four cases, it worked as a fail-safe device, getting us out of a situation which looked threatening at the time and which *might* have led to a serious fall in price. In *no* cases did it leave us holding a share which plummeted from what was the peak price at the time. We can expect no more from any selling indicator, and can, quite obviously, apply this indicator with confidence to our entire shareholding.

In Chapter 6 as well as the list of 30 shares recommended for buying in 1978, which we have just been discussing in terms of selling indicators, a second list was given as recommended buys for the market turning point of 9th March 1979. In order to show how consistent these selling indicators are, the results of applying them to this second list of shares are given in Table 7.13. As was the case for the 1978 shares, the rise – fall indicator gave a signal in all 30 cases, while the other two indicators did not. The 13-week moving average indicator gave no selling signals for MFI, Brown & Jackson and Wholesale Fittings. The 9-week low indicator gave no signal for these three shares and no signal for United Engineering. A glance through the columns headed 'gain (loss)' shows that, as was true of the 1978 list of shares, the rise – fall indicator was by far the best.

The low risk attached to buying shares and then selling according to this indicator is exemplified by the gains and losses shown for the rise – fall indicator. Out of the 30 shares involved, only seven showed a loss. The worst loss of these seven was 8.3% in the case of Bentima. The smallest loss was 1.2% in the case of Saga Holidays and the seven losing shares lost an average of 4.1%. Of the remaining 23, two showed neither a gain nor a loss. The 21 shares which gained showed gains of from 3.1% to 227.4%, averaging a rise of 32.2%. Thus the chances of picking a winner as opposed to a loser from this list are exactly three to one. Moreover, each winner averaged a gain of 32.2%, while each loser averaged a loss of only 4.1% All this can be restated as the chances of making a certain percentage gain to the chance of making the same percentage loss are about 96 to 4, or 24 to 1.

For the whole list of shares, the average gain achieved if they were bought on 9th March 1979 and sold according to the rise – fall indicator, would have been 20.5%. This is superior to the gain of 4.6% which would have been made by holding the shares for 12 months, as discussed in the last chapter. It is even more superior than one would think from these figures, since the average period for which we would have remained invested in these shares was just 7 weeks!

Looking through Table 7.13 again, one could quite rightly, perhaps, raise the point that the figures give a distorted view because of the presence of the high-flying share Brown & Jackson, which gained 227.4% in the period 9 March 1979 to 8 June 1979. One answer to this could be that a system which can catch these high flyers is obviously to be preferred to one which lets them get away. Another answer could be 'Let's see what the results would be if we left that one out'. By doing this, the average gain for the other 29 shares turns out to be 13.4% over the 7-week period. Thus the rise – fall indicator is still eminently successful.

As in the list of 30 shares given as good buys for 1978, the 1979 list should also be subjected to a test of how far from the peak price the rise – fall indicator told us to sell. The peak prices attained during the 6 month period 9th March 1979 to 7th September 1979, and the price at which the rise – fall indicator signalled, are given in Table 7.14. For the 30 shares in the table, the rise – fall indicator gave its signal at an average of 7.9% from the peak price attained during the period. The consistency of this indicator is remarkable, since the corresponding figure for the 1978 list of shares (see Table 7.12) is 7 – 8%!

Table 7.13. The selling signals, selling prices and appropriate gains and losses for the 30 strongest shares in Table 6.9 since the 9th March 1979

		13-week average indicator			*9-week low indicator*			*Rise – fall indicator*		
Share	*Price at 9 Mar. 79*	*Date*	*Price*	*Gain (loss)*	*Date*	*Price*	*Gain (loss)*	*Date*	*Price*	*Gain (loss)*
MFI*	122	—	160	31.1	—	160	31.1	24 Mar. 79	118	(3.3)
Status Disc.*	58¼	15 June 79	63	8.2	15 June 79	63	8.2	20 Apr. 79	77	32.2
Bambers*	90	6 July 79	134	48.9	29 June 79	129	43.3	15 June 79	142	57.8
Kode Internat.	226	8 June 79	218	(3.5)	1 June 79	214	(5.3)	31 Mar. 79	233	3.1
Lee Cooper*	173¼	13 July 79	187	7.9	27 July 79	178	2.7	19 May 79	198	14.3
Bullough	242	29 June 79	246	1.7	15 June 79	252	4.1	19 May 79	274	13.2
Hawtin	19¼	26 May 79	15	(22.1)	19 May 79	16¼	(15.6)	4 May 79	18¼	(5.2)
Caplan Profile*	128½	6 July 79	215	67.3	15 June 79	216	68.1	15 June 79	216	68.1
A.Arenson	120	20 July 79	120	0	15 June 79	118	(1.6)	31 Mar. 79	118	(1.7)
Meggitt	32	20 July 79	28	(12.5)	20 July 79	28	(12.5)	17 Mar. 79	32	0
Homecharm*	114	15 June 79	102	(10.5)	15 Apr. 79	102	(10.5)	13 Apr. 79	118	35.0
Mining Supp.*	81½	27 July 79	79	(3.1)	27 July 79	79	(3.1)	8 June 79	106	30.1
Vectis Stone*	30	15 June 79	26	(13.3)	26 May 79	29	(3.3)	13 Apr. 79	38	26.7
Metalrax*	58¼	6 July 79	55	(5.6)	15 June 79	56½	(3.0)	19 May 79	65	11.6
Gripperrods	94	29 June 79	122	29.7	1 June 79	116	23.4	19 May 79	120	27.7
Utd Engineering*	74½	10 Aug. 79	83	11.5	—	92	23.5	12 May 79	91½	22.8
Prince of W.Htl	125	6 Apr. 79	118	(5.6)	27 Apr. 79	113	(9.6)	24 Mar. 79	123	(1.6)
Brown & Jackson	70¼	—	270	284.3	—	270	284.3	8 June 79	230	227.4
Energy Services	25¾	11 May 79	29	12.6	25 May 79	26¾	3.9	20 Apr. 79	30	16.5
A.B.Electronic	208	22 June 79	192	(7.7)	1 June 79	204	(1.9)	31 Mar. 79	206	(1.0)
Whole.Fittings	300	—	402	34.0	—	402	34.0	8 June 79	355	18.3
G.Saville	43¼	22 June 79	39	(9.8)	1 June 79	43	(0.6)	13 Apr. 79	46	6.4
Dewhirst*	83¼	27 July 79	95	14.1	27 July 79	95	14.1	15 June 79	98¼	18.0

Table 7.13. (cont'd)

Share	Price at 9 Mar. 79	13-week average indicator			9-week low indicator			Rise – fall indicator		
		Date	Price	Gain (loss)	Date	Price	Gain (loss)	Date	Price	Gain (loss)
Electrocompns.	412	27 July 79	420	2.0	27 July 79	420	2.0	31 Mar. 79	428	3.9
Bentima	60	8 June 79	55	(8.3)	15 June 79	53	(11.7)	19 May 79	55	(8.3)
Boardman	28	8 June 79	24	(14.2)	12 May 79	24	(14.2)	20 Apr. 79	26	(7.1)
Brit. Benzole	44	22 June 79	43	(2.3)	7 Sept. 79	43	(2.3)	31 Mar. 79	44	1
J.Halstead	36	13 July 79	43	19.4	3 Aug. 79	42	16.7	12 May 79	44	22.2
Fed.Land	67	15 June 79	66	(1.5)	15 June 79	66	(1.5)	31 Mar. 79	81	20.8
Saga Holidays	236	19 May 79	178	(24.6)	20 Apr. 79	180	(23.7)	17 Mar. 79	233	(1.2)

Average gain for group 20.5%
Average period 7 weeks

*Scrip: where no signal is given, the price 6 months later at 7 Sept. 79 is given.

As was true of the 1978 shares, those shares for which the indicator appears to be less successful — MFI, Arenson, Meggitt, Gripperods, Brown & Jackson, AB Electronic, Wholesale Fittings and Bentima — are cases in which the share price dipped for a few weeks before proceeding upwards to even higher levels. The indicator gave its signal on the price dip and so cannot be considered to be unsatisfactory. As was pointed out previously, under such conditions the indicator errs on the side of safety, since the dip in the share price, later seen to have been of a temporary nature, may well have continued into a prolonged fall. In *no* case did a share price fall more than 10% down from its short-term peak price without the indicator being triggered.

Table 7.14. Rise – fall indicator

Share (from Table 7.13)	Peak price	Price when indicator signalled	% down from peak price
MFI*	164	118	28.0
Status Discount*	80	77	3.8
Bambers*	155	142	8.4
Kode International	236	233	1.3
Lee Cooper*	208	198	4.8
Bullough	274	274	0
Hawtin	19¼	18¼	5.2
Caplan Profile*	239	216	9.6
A.Arenson	132	118	10.6
Meggitt	39	32	17.9
Homecharm*	130	118	9.2
Mining Supplies*	108	106	1.9
Vectis Stone*	38	38	0
Metalrax*	68¼	65	4.8
Gripperrods	155	120	22.6
United Engineering*	92	91½	0.5
Prince of Wales Hotels	125	123	1.6
Brown & Jackson	300	230	23.3
Energy Services	30½	30	1.6
A.B.Electronic	242	206	14.8
Wholesale Fittings	402	355	11.7
G.Saville	48	46	4.2
Dewhirst*	105¾	98¼	7.1
Electrocomponents	450	428	4.9
Bentima	63	55	12.6
Boardman	28½	26	8.8
British Benzole	46½	44	5.4
J.Halstead	48½	44	9.2
Federated Land	82	81	1.2
Saga Holidays	235	233	0.9
		Average	7.9%

*Prices adjusted for scrip issues and/or splits.

In order to avoid repetition, data on these indicators for years prior to 1978 have not been given. However, in all cases the rise – fall indicator is superior to the moving average and 9-week low indicators. Over the 10-year period since 1970, the rise – fall indicator has consistently given selling signals between 5% and 9% down from the short-term peak price. Once some experience has been gained in the application of these three selling indicators discussed in this chapter, the rise – fall indicator can be followed exclusively. It should continue to perform in the future as it has done in the past, and should enable us to time our selling to around 7% to 8% down from the peak share price reached during that particular phase of the market.

Chapter 8

The Method in Practice

At this point in the book it is necessary to take stock of the methods we have developed so far in separate chapters, and show how they link together in one rounded package. We can also indicate the steps we have to take each weekend in order to keep on top of market developments, so that a reader could, from the information in this chapter alone, function as an investor who regularly out-performs the market, as measured by either the Financial Times Index or the All Share Index.

The essentials of the method are these:

1. We have developed a buying indicator which measures the state of the market and tells us to buy within a few weeks of the market climate changing for the better. This indicator has, over the last decade, consistently marked the beginning of upward surges in share prices that have lasted for at least a few months.
2. We have developed a method of choosing shares which, from the buying signal onwards, outperform the market in general.
3. We have developed an indicator to tell us when to sell the shares we have bought. Over the last decade this indicator has told us to sell when the share price has been an average of about 7–8% down from the peak price. About once in every four or five occasions the indicator gives a selling signal for a share which later recovers and moves to new heights. This is the price we pay for added safety, because this indicator has rarely allowed us to ride a share price down more than 10% from its peak price.

To show what we have to do each week in practice, we can assume that the market is falling when we commence the method. This allows us to pass through the above categories 1–3 consecutively.

MEASURING THE MARKET

(**Time**: 5 minutes each week)
Each week we keep a record of the Friday closing value of the Financial Times

Index and from these we can calculate a 5-week and 13-week moving average. The best method of recording this information, and later the information on individual share prices is to use A4 paper ruled into 5 mm squares, obtainable from any stationers. For the market index we can rule eight vertical columns headed 'Date', 'FT Index', '5-week take away', '5-week total', '5-week average', '13-week take away', '13-week total' and finally '13-week average'. The 'take away' columns need only be one square wide, since only crosses will be put into them to remind us which value of the index to subtract from the 5-week and 13-week running totals. All the other columns can be five squares wide. Figure 8.1 shows a typical record of this type. We cannot compute a 5-week average until we have recorded five weekly values of the FT Index, and we cannot compute a 13-week average until we have 13 weeks' values of the index.

The 5-week average is calculated as follows. Once we have five consecutive weeks' values of the Index, add these and put the total in the '5-week total' column on the same horizontal line as the week 5. Dividing this by 5 gives us the 5-week average, which is put in the appropriate column again opposite week 5. On the sixth week, we have to subtract the FT Index value for week 1 from this total, and add in the value for week 6. This is where the 'take away' column comes in. In this column, opposite week 1, i.e. the week which we have subtracted from the total, we put cross. Finally, the new running total 'week 5 total − week 1 index + week 6 index' goes into the '5-week total' column opposite week 6, and this total, divided by 5 goes into the '5-week average' column.

Next week, week 7, we take the latest running total, and subtract the FT Index after the one with a cross and add in the latest week 7 value of the Index, and just continue in this fashion.

DATE	FT INDEX	X	5 WK TOTAL	5 WK AVGE	X	13 WK TOTAL	13 WK AVGE
5·1·80	413·9	X	2086·1	417·2	X	5577·1	429·0
12·1·80	435·2	X	2106·1	421·2	X	5537·3	425·9
19·1·80	459·8	X	2146·3	428·6	X	5527·3	425·2
26·1·80	452·4	X	2179·1	435·8	X	5539·5	426·1
2·2·80	447·8	X	2209·1	441·8	X	5555·6	427·4
9·2·80	461·4	X	2256·6	451·2	X	5596·1	430·5
16·2·80	462·6	X	2284·0	456·8	X	5651·7	434·7
23·2·80	454·2	X	2278·4	455·6	X	5697·3	438·3
1·3·80	467·1	X	2293·1	458·6	X	5743·7	441·8
8·3·80	455·7	X	2301·0	460·2	X	5783·8	444·9
15·3·80	439·9	X	2279·5	455·8		5804·1	446·5
22·3·80	429·9	X	2246·8	449·2		5814·4	447·3
29·3·80	421·5	X	2214·1	442·8		5818·1	447·5
5·4·80	432·6	X	2179·6	435·9		5836·8	449·0
12·4·80	435·6	X	2159·5	431·8		5837·2	449·0
19·4·80	442·7	X	2169·3	432·4		5820·1	447·7
26·4·80	427·5	X	2159·9	431·8		5795·2	445·8
3·5·80	443·6	X	2182·0	436·4		5791·0	445·5
10·5·80	436·5		2186·0	437·2		5766·1	443·5
17·5·80	435·7		2186·0	437·2		5739·2	441·5
24·5·80	423·9		2166·6	433·3		5708·3	439·1
31·5·80	415·9		2155·0	431·0		5657·2	435·2
7·6·80	428·5		2134·9	426·0		5630·0	433·1

Figure 8.1. The weekly data kept on the Financial Times Index.

The 13-week average is calculated in exactly the same way, adding up the first 13 weeks' value of the Index to give the first total and average. On week 14 we take away the Index for week 1, put a cross in the '13-week take away' column, and add in the Index for week 14. Dividing this by 13 gives the 13-week average. This procedure is continued for subsequent weeks.

Depending on whether you think you are an aggressive investor or more cautious, your buying signal is given when either the 5-week average, which has been falling so far, turns upward, or when the 13-week average also turns upward.

DECIDING WHAT TO BUY

(a) Listing volatile shares
(**Time**: 1 – 2 hours, once during a falling market)
When the 13-week average has been falling some months, it is time to prepare a list of the 100 – 150 or so most volatile shares from all those in the *Financial Times* list of shares. Go through the columns marked '1979/80' or whichever year is recorded there 'high and low'. Underline all those shares which a mental calculation shows that the ratio of high to low prices is about 1.5 or more. If you have 100 – 150 such shares, all well and good, if many more, raise the required ratio to 1.6 or 1.7 as necessary to keep below 150. If the number is less than 100, lower the required ratio a little. This choosing operation should take no more than 30 minutes. The rest of the time comes in writing these shares down. Again, our 5 mm squared paper is useful for this. Rule it off vertically in columns headed 'share', '1979/80 high', '1979/80 low' (change the year as appropriate) 'Price at — ', 'Price at — as % of 1979/80 high'. This gives five columns, only three of which (share and high, low prices) we can use at the moment to write in the volatile shares we have chosen. The — will have the data entered when the market, as signalled by the indicator we are following, turns up.

(b) Choosing strong shares
(**Time**: 1 – 2 hours, once when the market indicator turns up)
Once the 5-week average or 13-week average of the Financial Times Index turns up — depending upon which you are using as your buying indicator — it is time to choose the strongest shares from the list of volatile shares. Enter into the list of volatile shares the prices for the week the average turns up. For each share, calculate its price as a percentage of the price in the 1979/80 (or whichever year is entered) 'high' column, and enter this value in the appropriate column.

If the market has not fallen very far from its previous high, quite a proportion of the shares in the list will show percentage values greater than 100%, whereas for a drastic fall in the market, only a few, or perhaps none, will have risen higher than their previous high.

Finally, make a list of the 30 strongest shares in this list. Your selection of five or six shares to buy is then made from this list.

DECIDING WHEN TO SELL

(**Time:** 15 minutes each week)
Once you have bought shares, continue to keep track of the FT Index by means of the 13-week moving average, since this is your guide to general market conditions. However, your main attention now turns to the performance of the shares you have bought. It will be necessary to keep track of three indicators, the 13-week average, 9-week low and the rise – fall indicator. By means of the 5 mm squared paper, all the data for a share can be collected on one sheet of paper. The paper can be ruled off in columns for 'Date', 'Price', '13-week take away', '13-week total', '13-week average' and '9-week low'. If these columns are kept to the left hand half of the page, the rise – fall indicator can be plotted on the

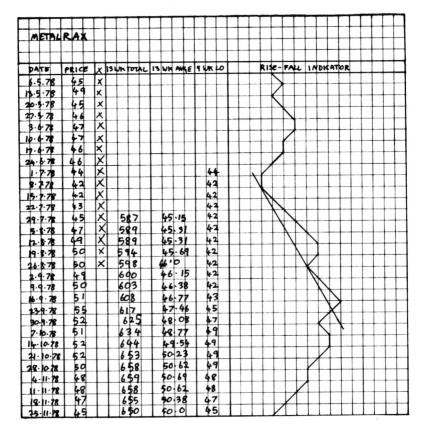

DATE	PRICE	X	13 WK TOTAL	13 WK AVGE	9 WK LO	RISE-FALL INDICATOR
6.5.78	45	X				
13.5.78	49	X				
20.5.78	45	X				
27.5.78	46	X				
3.6.78	47	X				
10.6.78	47	X				
17.6.78	46	X				
24.6.78	46	X				
1.7.78	44	X			44	
8.7.78	42	X			42	
15.7.78	42	X			42	
22.7.78	43	X			43	
29.7.78	45	X	587	45.15	42	
5.8.78	47	X	589	45.31	42	
12.8.78	49	X	589	45.31	42	
19.8.78	50	X	594	45.69	42	
26.8.78	50	X	598	46.0	42	
2.9.78	49		600	46.15	42	
9.9.78	50		603	46.38	42	
16.9.78	51		608	46.77	43	
23.9.78	55		617	47.46	45	
30.9.78	52		625	48.08	47	
7.10.78	51		634	48.77	49	
14.10.78	52		644	49.54	49	
21.10.78	52		653	50.23	49	
28.10.78	50		658	50.62	49	
4.11.78	48		659	50.69	48	
11.11.78	48		658	50.62	48	
18.11.78	47		655	50.38	47	
25.11.78	45		650	50.0	45	

Figure 8.2. The weekly data kept once a share has been bought.

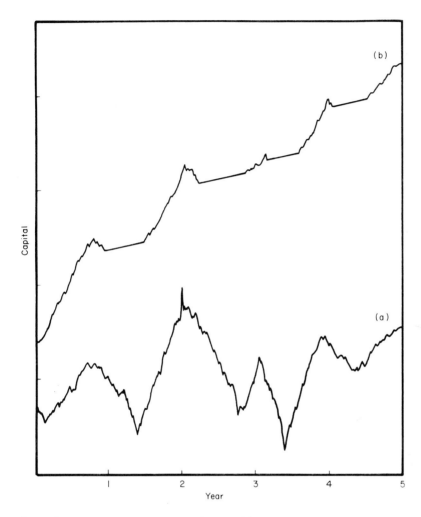

Figure 8.3. How we hope our capital will grow: (a) the behaviour of a typical stock market; (b) the behaviour of our investments over the same period of time.

right hand half of the paper. An example is shown in Fig. 8.2.

The 13-week average for the share is kept in exactly the same way as that for the FT Index. The 9-week low indicator simply means that each week we enter the lowest price that the share reached during the previous 9 weeks. The rise – fall indicator is started for the first week on the line for week 1, on one of the 5 mm ruled lines about halfway across the right hand half of the page. If the price falls the following week, draw a line to the next 5 mm square on the left, if the price rises, draw it to the right, while if the price remains the same, draw the line vertically down to the next ruled line. Figure 8.2 should make clear how this indicator is maintained. Once we have one or more 'saw teeth' we can draw a trend line through the bottom of the teeth.

Selling signals are generated when the 13-week average turns down, when the price drops lower than the lowest price in the last 9 weeks, and when the trend-line of the rise – fall indicator is violated on the downside.

The proceeds from sales of shares should not be reinvested in shares until the next turn up in the market is signalled by the 13-week moving average of the FT Index.

With the spread of microcomputers into all areas of life, these devices offer a way of not only reducing the time available to store the above information on shares but to retrieve the information rapidly. Two hundred or more shares can readily be kept track of weekly by this means. More information on their availability and programmes relevant to investors is given in Appendix E.

The overall effect we are aiming to achieve with this investment method is shown in Fig. 8.3. When the market is rising, we hope to be rising with it, giving us a large capital gain. Some of this will be lost by virtue of the fact that our selling indicators only tell us to sell when our shares have come off their tops. Our capital will then stand still, or gain at bank deposit or building society rates of interest if we do place it, while the market falls. On the next rise we step aboard again, and so on. It will not take too many such operations to double, treble or multiply by even more our original starting capital.

Chapter 9

What to do if the Market is Falling

The short answer to the question 'What should I do if the market is falling?' is 'Nothing!' Nothing, that is, besides collect data about the most volatile shares, and those amongst these volatile shares that are the strongest according to the rules outlined in the last chapter, and of course keep track of the 5-week and 13-week moving averages of the Financial Times Index in order to determine when to come into the market. If you are new to investment when you pick up this book, then undoubtedly you will be impatient to get started. After all, who wants to have to wait a year perhaps until the market rises again before making that first investment decision? If you really must take the plunge, there are several procedures which one can utilize to make investments in a falling market, but such investments are of necessity subject to higher risk than the methods which have been discussed so far in this book. This should be clearly understood, as should the fact that the procedures are not short term, so that one's money could be tied up for a number of years before a profit is there for the taking. If you have some money available now which you would like to invest but see yourself needing it next year or the year after to buy a new car, boat, or build that extension you have been after for so long, then skip this chapter, since you will find yourself having to sell your shares at the time when you are showing the greatest loss. Only if you have some uncommitted capital should you envisage applying the methods discussed in this chapter.

Besides money, one other thing that you should have available to supply at the outset is strong nerve, because you are going to be asked to invest a sum of money, watch the value of your investment go down, and then be asked to buy even more of the same shares. It sounds very much like throwing good money after bad. However, the type of share that we are going to invest is a cyclical one, that has fluctuated fairly widely in price on a fairly long time-scale, peaking out every 4 years or even longer. So, however badly it is doing at the moment, we can reasonably expect that some time in the not too distant future, the price is going to rise sufficiently to give us a profit. We wish to accumulate a large number of these shares when the price is falling, and the lower the price falls the better. The element of risk involved is the degree of uncertainty that the price will ever rise again above what we have paid for the shares. If it does not, then we will lose money. If they rise even higher than their previous peak, then we will make a very good profit. Bearing in mind the time-scale we are talking about, it could well be 4 or 5 years before we see that profit. Because of this long time interval, we should hope to achieve a profit of at least 100% over a 4-year period in order to improve on the methods developed in the previous chapters of this book.

Each of the methods illustrated here employs the principle of *cost averaging*. We have to buy shares at fixed time intervals which we decide on ourselves bearing in mind our cash flow situation. The prevailing share price at the allotted time must not affect our decision to buy — there must be no question of saying to ourselves, 'Why not wait another week or so because the price is going to move in our favour?' The buying must be completely automatic on the pre-determined date. Once we have carried out a number of such purchases, the cost per share to us will start to approach the average value at which they have stood over the period of time. If we happen to be buying when the actual price is below the average, then that will tend to decrease our cost per share even further, so giving us a greater potential for profit when the rise comes. Our profit starts to appear when the price of the share rises above the average price, or rather above the price per share which we have paid by then.

Before we commence one of these schemes of investment, we have to decide on two things: firstly, how much money we are going to have available over, say, the coming 4-year period, and secondly, which share we are going to buy.

As far as the money available is concerned, we should be buying our shares at a frequency of somewhere between 2 and 6 months, and we should bear in mind that it is not economical to invest less than about £150 at a time if commission is not to form an overly large percentage of the costs. So, the sort of investment that we have in mind is between say £300 and £1000 per year, over at least a 4-year period. As we emphasized earlier, this type of operation should not be undertaken unless these funds are totally uncommitted. The last thing we want to have to do is to realize our investment when share prices are low, and, life being what it is, share prices will be low when we need the money most.

The criteria for selecting the share are that it should have a history of cyclicality, and that it should be as 'safe' a company as possible — although since the Rolls-Royce affair it is apparent that there is no such thing as a safe company. It will be fairly easy to choose such a company by reference to Appendix D at the end of this book, where the 50 top companies in terms of turnover are given. The example used in this chapter is that of John Brown, the engineering company. Its cyclicality can be illustrated by the chart of its share price since 1972 given in Fig. A.19.

For the purposes of these calculations, we shall assume that an investment is made every 20 weeks, i.e. about every 5 months.

Method 1: buying a constant number of shares

In this method, we buy a fixed number of shares, for example 100, 200, 1000 as the case may be, each time our schedule says to buy. Applied to the shares of John Brown, we get the figures shown in Table 9.1. Columns in the table give us the number of shares bought to date and their cost to date, from which we calculate the most important fact, which is the cost per share to date. Other columns give us the market value to date, which is obtained by multiplying the number of shares held by their present market price. The difference between the market value and the amount we have paid to date gives us the gain or loss situation, expressed as a percentage. The buying scheme was started on 28th January 1972, and by 11th July 1975 we had bought 1000 shares, at a cost of £1182.00. However, at that time, the market value of the shares, then standing at 60p was only £600.00, so we were showing a loss of nearly 50% on our investment! That is the time for strong nerves, and is also a reason why we have said that we must not be in a position of needing this money and hence having to sell out at such a large loss. The system was vindicated by June 1977 when we moved into a profit. By May 1979, we had gained a very large profit indeed, our total expenditure of £3007.00 now being worth £10 640.00 showing a gain of 253.8% over the 7-year period from January 1972. In the figures presented here we have made no allowance for the commission involved in buying the share but have made the reasonable assumption that this would have been offset several times over by dividends received, so that the real gain would have been slightly higher that that shown.

This gain of 253% is far and away above that which we would have obtained by depositing the same sums in a building society or bank account over the same period of time. We could not have even doubled our money in the time by such means. So, on the basis of the example given here, cost averaging appears to be a very useful way of building up capital.

Before we rush off and start buying, though, let us look a little more closely at the John Brown situation. We started when the share price was 175p, and we calculated our profit on the selling price of 560p in 1979. We cannot expect too many shares to start with a certain price which rises to three times that at the end of 7 years. We can certainly hope to see some kind of rise because, as shown in Chapter 2, share prices are tending to rise over the long term. Of course there is just a chance that they may start to fall over the next 4 or 5 years, and so, to keep our perspective, we should look at the situation where the share price does not rise as high as the former peak. A convenient way of doing this is to generate an artificial share by reversing the prices of John Brown shares. We can say that the price started at 560p and ended at 175p. What happens by adopting the same investment procedure of buying 100 shares each time can be seen from Table 9.2. The value of our shares, accumulated through 19 forays into the market, is about 2% down on the amount we paid of them, excluding any consideration of commission.

This loss illustrates one of the major shortcomings of cost averaging where we buy a constant number of shares, which is that it does not succeed if the

Table 9.1. The long-term gain achieved by buying a constant number of shares in John Brown at constant intervals since 1972

Date	Price (p)	No bought	Cumulative cost (£)	Total no of shares held	Cost per share (p)	Value of investment (£)	Gain (loss)
28 Jan. 72	175	100	175	100	175	175	—
16 June 72	150	100	325	200	162.5	300	(7.7)
3 Nov. 72	135	100	460	300	153.3	405	(11.9)
23 Mar. 73	150	100	610	400	152.5	600	(1.6)
10 Aug. 73	155	100	675	500	153	775	1.3
28 Dec. 73	125	100	890	600	148.3	750	(15.7)
17 Mar. 74	73	100	963	700	137.6	511	(46.9)
4 Oct. 74	77	100	1040	800	130	616	(40.8)
21 Feb. 75	82	100	1122	900	124.7	738	(34.2)
11 July 75	60	100	1182	1000	118.2	600	(49.2)
28 Nov. 75	60	100	1242	1100	112.9	660	(46.9)
16 Apr. 76	87	100	1329	1200	110.75	1 044	(21.4)
3 Sept. 76	90	100	1419	1300	109.2	1 170	(17.5)
21 Jan. 77	102	100	1521	1400	108.6	1 428	(6.1)
10 June 77	200	100	1721	1500	114	3 000	74.3
28 Oct. 77	208	100	1926	1600	120	3 280	70.3
17 Mar. 78	276	100	2202	1700	124.5	4 692	113.1
4 Aug. 78	430	100	2632	1800	146.2	7 740	194.1
22 Dec. 78	375	100	3007	1900	158.3	7 125	136.9
11 May 79	560	100	3007	1900	158.3	10 640	253.8

Table 9.2. The long-term loss achieved by buying a constant number of shares in a mythical share ('reverse' John Brown) at constant intervals since 1972

Price (p)	No bought	Cumulative cost (£)	Total no of shares held	Cost per share (p)	Value of investment (£)	Gain (loss)
560	100	560	100	560	560	—
375	100	935	200	467.5	750	(19.8)
430	100	1365	300	455	1290	(5.5)
276	100	1641	400	410.3	1104	(32.7)
205	100	1846	500	369.2	1025	(44.5)
200	100	2046	600	341.0	1200	(41.3)
102	100	2148	700	306.4	714	(66.8)
90	100	2238	800	279.8	720	(67.8)
87	100	2325	900	258.3	783	(66.3)
60	100	2385	1000	238.3	600	(74.8)
60	100	2445	1100	222.3	660	(73.0)
82	100	2527	1200	210.6	984	(61.1)
77	100	2604	1300	200.3	1001	(61.6)
73	100	2677	1400	191.2	1022	(61.8)
125	100	2802	1500	186.8	1875	(33.1)
155	100	2957	1600	184.8	2480	(16.1)
150	100	3107	1700	182.8	2550	(17.9)
135	100	3242	1800	180.1	2430	(25.0)
150	100	3392	1900	178.5	2850	(16.0)
175	—	3392	1900	178.5	3325	(2.0)

long-term underlying trend of the share price is downwards. The reason for this is that the procedure we have adopted is simply giving us an arithmetical average of the share price, and of course, when the long-term trend is downwards, it is a mathematical necessity that the average share price is going to fall. The only chance we might have to make a profit in such situations is if the share price spurts above this average for a short term. If it does, we would be advised to terminate the scheme of investment.

Method 2: buying with a constant sum of money

The key to success in cost averaging operations is to lower the cost per share which we have paid, i.e. our total expenditure divided by the number of shares we have accumulated at the time. The obvious way to do this is to buy more shares when prices are low than when they are high. This can be done quite simply by, instead of buying a fixed number of shares each time, as in the last method, investing a *fixed sum* each time. Thus if the price of the share drops to half its previous value, we will be able to buy twice as many.

As far as the examples which we have chosen to illustrate the method are concerned, they are somewhat artificial in the sense that such an exercise will result in buying odd numbers of shares, such as 189. Brokers do not take too kindly to this, and much prefer round hundreds, although they are not too upset at multiples of 50. However, we can ignore this factor for the moment since we only intend to illustrate the advantages of fixed sum investment over fixed number investment.

In order to come somewhere near the last example in terms of the total amount of money invested, we will base our calculations on fixed investments of £200. The results are shown in Table 9.3. The figures are extremely impressive, showing that £3800 invested in John Brown shares by this procedure become worth £18362 by May 1979 when the share price was standing at 560p. This represents a gain of 382% for the period, which is over half as much again as the previous method yielded.

The crucial point about this second method of investment is not so much how it performs on John Brown shares relative to the first method, but how well it would perform on the 'reverse John Brown' shares, which started off at a high level and then failed to come up to that on the recovery. The answer, as can be seen from Table 9.4, is that this method produces a gain of 47.4% for the 7-year period. This is quite a turn around from the 2% loss produced by the first method, and shows that the investment of a *fixed sum* of money rather than the buying of a *fixed number* of shares is the way to success with a cost averaging system. Having found an improved system for cost averaging, we might ask ourselves if the improved method can be improved even further. Since the aim in any system is to reduce the cost per share of our accumulated holding, this is the area to look at. The second method was an improvement over the first method because it resulted in the purchase of more shares when prices were low than when they were high. To do even better, we need to buy an even greater

Table 9.3. The long-term gain achieved by investing a fixed amount of money in John Brown shares since 1972

Date	Price (p)	Amount invested (£)	Cumulative cost (£)	No bought	Total no held	Cost per share (p)	Value of investment (£)	Gain (loss)
28 Jan. 72	175	200	200	114	114	175	175	—
16 June 72	150	200	400	133	247	161.9	370.5	(7.4)
3 Nov. 72	135	200	600	148	395	151.9	533.3	(11.1)
23 Mar. 73	150	200	800	133	528	151.5	792	(1.0)
10 Apr. 73	155	200	1000	129	657	156.2	1 018.4	1.8
28 Dec. 73	125	200	1200	160	817	146.9	1 021.3	(14.9)
17 May. 74	73	200	1400	274	1091	128.3	796.4	(43.1)
4 Oct. 74	77	200	1600	260	1351	118.4	1 040	(35)
21 Feb. 75	82	200	1800	244	1595	112.9	1 307.9	(27.3)
11 July 75	60	200	2000	333	1928	103.7	1 156.8	(42.2)
28 Nov. 75	60	200	2200	333	2261	97.3	1 356.6	(38.3)
16 Apr. 76	87	200	2400	230	2491	96.3	2 167.2	(9.7)
3 Sept. 76	90	200	2600	222	2713	95.8	2 441.7	(6.1)
21 Jan. 77	102	200	2800	196	2909	96.2	2 967.2	(6.0)
10 June 77	200	200	3000	100	3009	99.7	6 018	100.6
28 Oct. 77	208	200	3200	98	3107	103.0	6 369.4	89.0
17 Mar. 78	276	200	3400	72	3179	106.9	8 774	158.1
4 Aug. 78	430	200	3600	47	3226	111.6	13 871.8	285.3
22 Dec. 78	375	200	3800	53	3279	115.9	12 296.3	223.6
11 May. 79	560	—	3800	—	3279	115.9	18 362	383.2

Table 9.4. The long-term gain achieved by investing a fixed amount of money in a mythical share ('reverse' John Brown) at constant intervals since 1972

Price (p)	Amount invested (£)	No bought	Cumulative cost (£)	Total no of shares held	Cost per share (p)	Value of investment (£)	Gain (loss)
560	200	36	200	36	555	201	—
375	200	53	400	89	449	334	(16.5)
430	200	47	600	136	441	584.8	(2.5)
276	200	72	800	208	384	574.1	(28.2)
205	200	98	1000	306	327	627.3	(37.3)
200	200	100	1200	406	296	812	(32)
102	200	196	1400	602	233	614	(56.1)
90	200	222	1600	824	194	741.6	(53.7)
87	200	230	1800	1054	171	917	(49.1)
60	200	333	2000	1387	144	382.2	(58.4)
60	200	333	2200	1720	128	1032	(53.1)
82	200	244	2400	1964	122	1610.4	(32.9)
77	200	260	2600	2224	117	1712.5	(34.1)
73	200	274	2800	2498	112	1823.5	(34.9)
125	200	160	3000	2658	113	3322.5	10.8
155	200	129	3200	2787	115	4319.9	35
150	200	133	3400	2920	116	4380	28.8
135	200	148	3600	3068	117	4141.8	15.1
150	200	133	3800	3201	119	4801.5	26.4
175	200	—	3800	3201	119	5601.8	47.4

number of shares when prices are low. This will need extra money, and this extra money can come from the purchase of fewer shares when prices are high than was the case with the last method. So, instead of investing say £200 when prices are high, we should put in perhaps £150, and put the remaining £50 into a reserve fund. We can then use this reserve to spend more than £200 when prices are low. The only further point to be decided is how to calculate how many shares to buy each time we have to invest. A good way of doing this is to link the share price itself with our accumulated cost per share, so that if our cost per share is substantially higher than the current share price, we buy a larger number of shares in order to reduce it. Conversely, if the accumulated cost per share is lower than the current share price, then any purchase will raise our cost per share. Since our policy is also to accumulate as many shares as we can, we will have to buy a few shares in such a situation, but the number will be kept low. The basis of this method will be therefore to decide upon a certain amount to invest each time, and use only a part of it when prices are high, but supplement it from the reserve we build up to buy many more shares when prices are low.

Method 3: relating amount invested to share price movements

Since we are going to start this exercise when prices are falling, at least in the case of John Brown shares, then of course we need a reserve fund before we start. This can be done by putting £500 into the reserve, and using only £100 for the first purchase, putting the next £100 into the reserve as well, so that the latter stands at £500 for the second purchase. The simplest way of deciding how much to invest at the second purchase is to use ratio of our current cost per share (for the second purchase this will be the share price at the time of the first purchase) to the current share price. All these transactions are shown in detail in Table 9.5. In order to clarify matters we will go through the first few buying operations.

Initially we buy £100 worth of shares at 175p. This buys us 57 shares. The remaining £100 of our planned £200 per time investment is added to the reserve, bringing it up to £600. For the second purchase, we use the ratio of the cost per share so far to the new share price to tell us how much to invest. The ratio of the cost per share to the second share price is 175 to 150, i.e. 1.16. So, we invest 1.16 × £200 = £232 for the second purchase. Since we plan to invest £200 each month, the extra £32 comes from the reserve.

To show a situation where we add to the reserve, we can look at the two points when the share prices were 276p and 430p. When the price was 276p, the cost per share was 93.2p. The ratio of 93.2p to 430p is 0.215. Hence 0.215 × £200 = £43 was invested. By proceeding in this way, the method gave a gain of 406.6% over the same period as was covered in the other methods of investment.

As far as our 'reverse' John Brown shares are concerned, the method is more successful than the previous ones, resulting in a gain of 87.5% (Table 9.6).

Table 9.5. The long-term gain obtained by investing a proportion of a £200 repetitive amount in John Brown shares and putting the residue into a reserve (the proportion is determined by the change in share price)

Price	Factor	Amount invested (£)	No of shares bought	Total no held	Total cost (£)	Cost per share (p)	Reserve (£)	Value of reserve + shares	Gain (loss)
—	—	—	—	—	—	—	500	500	—
175	—	100	57	57	100	175	600	700	—
150	1.16	232	155	212	332	156.6	568	886	(1.5)
135	1.16	232	172	384	564	146.9	536	1 054.4	(4.1)
150	0.98	196	130	514	760	147.9	540	1 043.7	(19.7)
155	0.96	191	123	637	951	149.3	549	1 536.4	2.4
125	1.07	214	171	808	1165	144.2	535	1 545	(9.1)
73	1.81	361	494	1302	1526	117.2	374	1 324.5	(30.3)
77	1.42	284	370	1672	1810	108.3	290	1 577.4	(24.9)
82	1.25	250	304	1976	2060	104.3	240	1 860.3	(19.1)
60	1.65	330	551	2527	2390	94.6	110	1 626.2	(34.9)
60	1.51	302	503	3030	2692	88.8	8	1 826	(32.4)
87	0.98	196	225	3255	2888	88.7	12	2 843.9	(1.9)
90	0.95	190	211	3466	3078	88.8	22	3 141.4	1.3
102	0.84	168	164	3630	3246	89.4	54	3 756.6	13.8
200	0.43	87	43	3673	3333	90.7	167	7 513	114.7
205	0.43	87	42	3715	3420	92.1	280	7 895.8	113.4
276	0.32	64	23	3738	3484	93.2	416	10 732.9	175.2
430	0.21	43	10	3748	3527	94.1	573	16 689.4	307.1
375	0.24	49	13	3761	3576	95.1	724	14 827.8	244.8
560	—	—	—	3761	3576	95.1	724	21 785.6	406.6

Table 9.6. The long-term gain obtained by investing a proportion of a £200 repetitive amount in mythical share ('reverse' John Brown) and putting the residue into a reverse (the proportion is determined by the change in share price)

Price	Factor	Amount invested (£)	No of shares bought	Total no held	Total cost (£)	Cost per share (p)	Reserve (£)	Value of reserve + shares	Gain (loss)
—	—	—	—	—	—	—	500	500	—
560	—	100	18	18	100	560	600	700	—
375	1.49	300	80	98	400	408	500	867.5	(3.6)
430	0.95	190	44	142	590	415	510	1 120.6	1.8
276	1.50	300	109	251	890	354.6	410	1 102.8	(15.2)
205	1.73	344	168	419	1234	294	266	1 124.9	(25)
200	1.47	294	147	566	1528	270	172	1 304	(23.9)
102	2.64	527	517	1083	2318	214	−155	949.7	(50)
90	2.38	475	528	1611	2793	173.4	−430	1 010	(51.9)
87	1.99	398	458	2069	3191	154.2	−628	1 172	(49)
60	2.57	514	857	2926	3705	126.6	−942	813.6	(67.5)
60	2.11	422	703	3629	4127	113.7	−1164	1 013.4	(62.5)
82	1.38	277	338	3967	4404	111	−1241	2 011.9	(30.6)
77	1.44	288	374	4341	4692	108.1	−1329	2 013.6	(35.0)
73	1.48	296	406	4747	4988	105.1	−1425	2 040.3	(38.2)
125	0.84	168	134	4881	5156	105.6	−1393	4 708.3	34.5
155	0.68	136	88	4969	5292	106.5	−1329	6 372.9	72.2
150	0.71	143	95	5064	5435	107.3	−1272	6 324	62.2
135	0.79	159	118	5182	5594	108	−1231	5 764.7	40.6
150	0.72	144	96	5278	5738	108.7	−1175	6 742	56.9
175	—	—	—	5278	5738	108.7	−1175	8 061.5	87.5

Besides the gains achieved by these various methods, another point of concern is how large the loss gets during the investment period before it turns into a profit. In the case of the 'ordinary' John Brown shares, the lowest points were for method 1, −49.2%, for method 2, −42.2%, and for method 3, −34.9%. So, as well as giving a superior gain for John Brown, method 3 also limited the loss during the time the shares were falling. For the 'reverse' John Brown shares, method 1 gave a maximum loss of 74.8%, method 2, 58.4% and method 3, 67.5%, so that method 3 came somewhere between methods 1 and 2 in this case. Comparison of the gains obtained with the three methods are John Brown and 'reverse' John Brown shares.

The gains for both types of share for each of the three methods are summarized in Table 9.7. Also shown is an average gain for the two types of shares, since perhaps we could consider this to approximate to a typical share. It can be seen that on all counts method 3 is superior, and so is to be preferred as a method of investment.

Table 9.7.

	Method 1 (%)	Method 2 (%)	Method 3 (%)
John Brown	253.8	383.2	406.6
'Reverse' John Brown	− 2.0	47.4	87.5
'Average' share	125.9	215.3	247.0

We have already mentioned the problem of buying shares in odd numbers rather than multiples of 50 or 100, and of course this would be one of the problems of applying method 3, since by its nature it will signal the purchase of odd numbers of shares. The only way around this problem is to round the number of shares calculated, either up or down to the nearest 50. If the factor works out at more than 1.0, then the number could be rounded upwards, whereas if it is less than 1.0, it can be rounded downwards. This has the effect of allowing the purchase of even more shares when the price is falling, and less when the price is rising, thereby decreasing the cost per share to a greater extent than is shown in Tables 9.5 and 9.6. By this means, the gains obtained will be greater than those we have illustrated in Tables 9.5 and 9.6.

Chapter 10

Options

Once you have had a number of successful forays into the market, one aspect will probably start to irritate you. This is that the rewards for being right in your investment decisions are not all that high. Your timing may be perfect as far as finding the bottom of the market and the top of your share price are concerned, but your selection of shares, although outperforming the market, are unlikely to include, unless you are extremely lucky, those that rack up gains of hundreds of per cent in a year or less. There is no way of finding these super-shares, one recent example of which has been Brown & Jackson, in which an investor putting in a few thousand pounds a year or so would now be sitting on a six figure investment. By the straightforward techniques we have been discussing in this book so far, we will probably achieve gains of between 50 and 100% in those bull markets which we have talked about. There is a way, however, in which being right can result in huge gains, although the opposite is also true, that being wrong will cost you more than simply buying and selling shares, and that is in the options market, particularly the traded options market which has been in existence in London since 1978.

Excluding traded options for the moment, standard options are of two types, 'put' options and 'call' options. A call option gives the right to buy, and a put option the right to sell at a specific price within a certain time period. This is usually 1, 2 or 3 months. Besides single options, which are either put or call, one can take out a double option, giving the right to buy or sell.

The 'striking price' which is the price at which the security can be bought or sold between now and the future expiry date is usually the present market price plus a few per cent more. The cost of taking out the option would be, in the case of a 3-month option typically 10 to 15%. As examples, the share price followed by the 3-month call rate in parentheses for some selected shares at the time of writing are as follows:

Babcock, 154 (18); Barclays, 440 (32); EMI, 97 ½ (12); Glaxo, 435 (50); ICI, 342 (24); Marks & Spencer, 119 (11); and Unilever, 508 (55).

The option can be taken up at any time within the specified period, or alternatively you can do nothing, in which case the option lapses and you lose the money which you paid for it. The share price will have to rise or fall by an amount sufficient to clear all these costs before you make a profit by exercising the option. The great advantage of options is that they enable you to take a position in the market at limited expense, and the rewards can be considerable if the correct view of the market's behaviour in the coming months has been taken.

In this chapter we will be concerned with traded options. In this particular market, one can actually sell the option itself, so that in fact the option has a market value which is constantly changing as the share price changes. Options give us a high leverage or gearing on our investment, in the sense that say a 20% rise in the share price can raise the value of the option by several hundred per cent. Obviously the rewards for being right are substantially higher than in the normal buying and selling of the shares themselves. Of course, leverage works both ways, so that you will have an increased loss if your view of the market is wrong. There are two ways of looking at this kind of leverage. If you are an out and out gambler, you could commit as much money in the options market as you might have put into shares. You may then make several hundreds percentage gain if you are correct, or, of course, you can lose the lot. The other, more sensible, way of looking at it is that you can commit only a fraction of your available funds, and still hope to make as much profit as if you had invested the whole of your capital in the purchase of shares. It is this latter view of options that we are advocating in this chapter, and we will not be committing anything like the sums of money that we would be putting into the straightforward dealing in shares. After all, if your timing and selection go badly wrong and your shares fall substantially, you still have some prospect that eventually they will come back in value, even though it might take a year or more. While that is happening you could adopt the philosophical attitude that your losses are only paper ones. With options, because of the limited time element, we have no such prospect, so our losses are real ones.

One valuable aspect of options, which we shall see shortly, is that they enable you to either increase or decrease the risk to your portfolio, and so traded options are going to be a valuable part of our investment techniques.

The traded options market is limited to the shares of 15 companies, which are listed in Table 10.1. Dealings in these options concern contracts, a contract giving the right to buy 1000 shares of the particular company at a fixed price. The options are designated by a month and a price, for example Marks & Spencer, January 100. At the time of writing (September) 1979 this gives the purchaser the right to buy, for each contract, 1000 shares in Marks & Spencer at any time between now and January 1980, at a price of 100p each. At any one time there are always three different expiry months available, for example Marks & Spencer, October, January and April, so that these are 3 months apart. Once we reach October, that option expires, and a new option appears called the July option. When a new option appears, it is always for 9 months ahead, and no longer term ones are available on the traded options market. The options are continually rolling over, so that in 3 months time, what is now a 3-month option, expires, the 6-month one will have become a 3-month option and the present 9 month becomes a 6 month, with a new 9-month option being

Table 10.1. Companies whose shares are quoted on the traded options market

Company	Months that new 9-month options are introduced			
British Petroleum	January	April	July	October
Commercial Union	January	April	July	October
Consolidated Gold	January	April	July	October
Courtaulds	January	April	July	October
GEC	January	April	July	October
Grand Metropolitan	January	April	July	October
ICI	January	April	July	October
Land Securities	January	April	July	October
Marks & Spencer	January	April	July	October
Shell Transport	January	April	July	October
BOC International*	February	May	August	November
Boots*	February	May	August	November
EMI*	February	May	August	November
Imperial Group	February	May	August	November
Rio Tinto Zinc	February	May	August	November

* Now replaced by Lonrho, P & O and Racal.

introduced. As shown in Table 10.1, ten companies have options introduced in February, May, August and November.

As far as the striking prices — sometimes called the exercise prices — are concerned, there will be, at the time of issue, some prices below the share price prevailing at the time, and some prices above the share price. If a share moves up or down a considerable amount, some of the prices will be discontinued as being inappropriate when next a new option is introduced. When we put together a company, a month and an exercise price, that is called a series. To use Marks & Spencer as an example, in August 1979, the following series were available: October 80, October 90, October 100, October 110, January 110, April 110, October 120, January 120, April 120, October 130, January 130, April 130. At the time, the actual share price fluctuated between 110p and 120p.

The prices of all these available series of options are given in those newspapers that carry extensive lists of share prices, and for a particular share, the prices will be different for each series. The further ahead the expiry date of the option, the more expensive it will be compared with earlier dates options, since it is assumed that the greater length of time available will give the buyer a better chance of the share price moving ahead. The lower the striking price of an option, the higher will be the price of a contract. Thus the cheapest contract on any particular day should be the short-term, high-striking price series, while the most expensive should be the low-striking price, long-term series.

Two expressions which are used in discussions of options are 'in the money' and 'out of the money'. In the money means that the striking price when you take out the option is lower than the actual share price. Because of this, at the time of purchase not all of the money you have paid for the contract is at risk.

Out of the money means that the striking price is above the current share price, and so all of your money is at risk. Hence out of the money contracts are more highly speculative than in the money ones, but naturally will be more highly geared.

So far we have only discussed the buying of contracts, but obviously, since we have a market, we must have sellers as well as buyers. The sellers are called writers of options, and they undertake to deliver the shares to you at the striking price if you exercise the option. As a writer you would receive the contract price less dealing costs. Of course you would only do this if you expected the share price to go down below the striking price, in which circumstance the holder of the option would not exercise it. So that we do not have situations where the writers of options cannot deliver the shares, writers have to lodge a margin with the market of either a quarter of the shares concerned, or the cash equivalent. So, as long as you deposit the cash, you do not actually have to have the shares, and you are what is known as a naked writer, as opposed to the covered writers who do have the shares. To be a naked writer is a dangerous state of affairs, since a dramatic rise in the share price would mean that the option would eventually be exercised, and you would have the problem of needing to buy the necessary shares at the much higher price.

We mentioned earlier that options can be used to reduce the risk to your portfolio. They can do this in the sense that we can take one view of the market as far as our shareholding is concerned, but cover ourselves for the market moving the other way by buying or writing options. Thus, supposing we think that the market is going to fall, we could liquidate our investments, but buy options with, say, 5 – 10% of the proceeds. If the market then rises, we can then come in at the cheap prices by exercising the options, or at least sell the options to increase our capital. On the other hand, if we think the market is going to rise, but wish to cover ourselves for a fall, we have at least made some money in the form of the payment we received for the contracts. Unfortunately, the taxman does not recognize this laudable aspect of options, and does not allow you to carry a loss forward against profits. He is very happy, however, to tax you on your profits.

Since we hope that by the timing methods discussed in the last chapter we will more often be correct than not about our view of the market, then it is unlikely that we would need to look at options as a means of neutralizing risk. To us they will be a means of increasing our profits when all the signals say that the market is taking off.

In Chapter 5 we pointed out that a buying signal was given by the 13-week average on 9th March 1979. Since the market peaked out on 4th May, it will be useful to compare the movement of a share price and the option prices in that share to a point just after the peak, say the week ending 11th May. The share prices and the offer prices of these option series which ran right through the period in question are given in Table 10.2. The extra leverage given by options is readily seen from the figures. It is worth commenting upon specific figures for the best and worst performing shares during the period in order to see if we can draw any conclusions. The best performing share was Marks & Spencer,

Table 10.2. Share prices and offer prices on 9th March 1979 and 11th May 1979 on various series on the traded options market

Share	Ex price	July option price 9 Mar. 79	July option price 11 May 79	% gain (loss)	October option price 9 Mar. 79	October option price 11 May 79	% gain	Share price 9 Mar. 79	Share price 11 May 79	% gain (loss)
BP	950	182	242	33.0	200	260	30.0	£11⅛	£12⅜	11.2
	1000	142	192	35.2	162	215	32.7			
	1050	104	142	36.5	128	172	34.4			
	1100	74	108	45.9	98	128	30.6			
Commercial Union	160	14½	26		20	29		168	170	4.8
	180	7	9		11	12				
Consolidated Gold	180	42	75	78.6	48	78	62.5	211	248	17.5
	200	27	55	103.7	35	58	65.7			
	220	18	35	94.4	23	46	100			
Courtaulds	100	18½	12		20	15		113	107	(5.3)
	110	11	7½		13½	9½				
	120	6	4½		9	6½				
	130	4	—		—	—	—			
GEC	330	66	124	87.9	76	142	86.8	382	435	13.9
	360	45	97	115.6	56	115	105.4			
	390	26	71	173.1	38	89	134.2			
Grand Metropolitan	100	45½	68	69.5	47½	70	47.3	140	162	15.7
	110	36	58	61.1	38	60	57.9			
	120	27	48	77.8	29½	50	69.5			
	130	19	38	100	22	40	81.8			
	140	13	29	123.1	18½	32	73.0			

Table 10.2. *(cont'd)*

Share	Ex price	July option price 9 Mar. 79	July option price 11 May 79	% gain (loss)	October option price 9 Mar. 79	October option price 11 May 79	% gain (loss)	Share price 9 Mar. 79	Share price 11 May 79	% gain (loss)
ICI	330	89	78	36	94	85		404	396	(1.9)
	360	61	48		65	58				
	390	37	26		45	37				
	420	18½	12		25	20				
Land Securities	240	57	78	36.8	65	88	35.4	287	308	7.3
	260	41	58	41.5	48	69	43.8			
	280	26	41	57.7	34	53	58.9			
	300	15	25	66.7	23	42	82.6			
Marks & Spencer	80	26	47	80.8	28	50	78.6	101	123	21.8
	90	17	37	117.6	19	40	110.5			
	100	10½	27	157.1	12	30	150			
Shell Transport	550	165	243		170	–		698	764	9.5
	600	115	193		125	207				
	650	75	143		92	157				
	700	43	95		53	112				

Share	Ex price	May option price 9 Mar. 79	May option price 11 May 79	% gain (loss)	August option price 9 Mar. 79	August option price 11 May 79	% gain (loss)	November option price 9 Mar. 79	November option price 11 May 79	% gain (loss)
BOC	60	17½	20½	17.1	18½	24	29.7	–	–	–
	70	8½	11	29.4	9½	15½	63.2	11	20	81.8
	80	2	2½	25.0	5	9	80	7	11½	64.3

Share price 75 (9 Mar. 79), 79½ (11 May 79) = 6.0% gain

Table 10.2. (cont'd)

Share	Ex price	July option price 9 Mar. 79	July option price 11 May 79	% gain (loss)	October option price 9 Mar. 79	October option price 11 May 79	% gain (loss)	Share price 9 Mar. 79	Share price 11 May 79	% gain (loss)
Boots	180	42	46		45	—	—	51	—	—
	200	24	26		29	33		36	42	
	220	11½	9		17½	19		25	28	
	240	4	2		—	10		—	19	
	260	2	1		—	—		—	—	
Share price 215 (9 Mar. 79), 224 (11 May 79) = 4.2% gain										
EMI	110	18	6	(66.7)	22	12	−45.5	26	16	(38.5)
	120	11	3	(72.7)	16	8	−50.0	21	12	(42.9)
	130	7	1	(85.7)	11	6	−45.5	16	10	(60.0)
	140	4	¼	(93.8)	8	4½	−43.75	12	9	(75.0)
Share price 120 (9 Mar. 79), 105 (11 May 79) = 12.5% loss										
Imperial Group	80	22½	23½		25	27		26½	29½	
	90	13	14½		15½	18½		17	21	
	100	7	4½		8½	9		10½	12	
Share price 120 (9 Mar. 79), 105 (11 May 79) = 12.5% loss										
RTZ	260	57	—	—	62	95	53.2	—	—	—
	280	39	54	38.5	49	78	59.2	58	99	
	300	24	34	41.7	38	62	63.2	46	84	
Share price 308 (9 Mar. 79), 332 (11 May 79) = 7.8% gain										

whose share price rose from 101p to 123p for a gain of 21.8%. By comparison, the best performing option series was the Marks & Spencer July 100s which moved from 10 ½p to 27p for a gain of 157.1% The least successful Marks & Spencer series was the October 80s which rose from 28p to 50p for a gain of 78.6%. The average gain for the six Marks & Spencer series was 115.8%. So, in the most favourable case amongst these options, the gain obtained from investing in them, was about seven times as high as if we had bought and sold the shares themselves.

As far as the worst performing share was concerned, this was EMI, whose share price fell from 120p to 105p, i.e. a loss of 12.5%. The heaviest losing option series was the November 110 series, losing 38.5%. The average loss for the twelve series was 60.0%, about five times the loss which would have been suffered by transactions in the share themselves. This should serve to remind us of the fact that high gearing works both ways — in forward and reverse.

Of course, losses such as these only become meaningful if we have no way of selecting in advance those shares which are going to be successful and those which are not when the market starts to climb. We have already formulated a successful selection procedure when we are given a choice of all the shares available on the market, so it would be interesting to test this procedure on the limited number of 15 shares which are all that are available to us in the traded options market. Remember our criteria were high volatility and strength in a falling market. When we chose our list in Chapter 6, we used the volatility, in terms of the ratio of the 1977/78 high to the 1977/78 low as at 12th January 1979, during the falling market. We then calculated the strength of the shares by seeing how far they had risen or fallen from their previous peak (the 1977/78 high) on 9th March 1979, when the buying signal was given. If we carry out the same operations on the 15 shares in the traded options market, we get the data given in Table 10.3. What we are trying to get from these data is a correlation between the gains and losses in the share price between 9th March 1979 and 11th May 1979 and the figures for volatility and strength. One obvious point that is pleasing is that the worst performing share, EMI, with a 12.5% loss is also the weakest, with a strength of 63.2%, i.e. its price at 9th March 1979 was only 63.2% of its previous peak in 1977/78, so naturally we would not have bought options in such a share.

Table 10.3 shows that the average volatility, in terms of the ratio of the 1977/78 high/low values, was 1.33 and the average strength was 103.0%, which means that the average share had risen 3% from its previous high value. Since we have already advocated volatility and strength as being of paramount importance a simple selection device is to choose those shares which are average or better both for strength and volatility, i.e. those shares whose strength is 103% or better, and whose volatility is also 1.33 or better. This procedure gives the six shares shown in Table 10.4.

The results show that this is a good method of selection, since the average gain in the share price of this group of six was 12.95%, just about double the gain in the original list of 15 shares. Not only that, but the procedure pulled in the best performer of the bunch, Marks & Spencer, and four out of the top five

Table 10.3. The traded options market

Share	1977/78 Low	High	Volatility (high/low)	Price at 9 Mar. 79	Strength (% of 77/78 high)	% gain (loss) at 11 May 79
BP	720	954	1.33	1112.5	116.6	11.2
Commercial U.	132	164	1.24	168	102.4	4.8
Consol.Gold	163	204	1.25	211	103.4	17.5
Courtaulds	109	131	1.20	113	86.3	(5.3)
GEC	233	349	1.5	382	109.5	13.9
Grand Met.	87	121	1.39	140	115.7	15.7
ICI	328	421	1.28	404	96.0	(1.9)
Land Secs	190	253	1.33	287	113.4	7.3
M & S	67½	94	1.39	101	107.4	21.8
Shell	484	602	1.24	698	115.9	9.5
BOC	63	79	1.25	75	94.9	6.0
Boots	184	237	1.29	215	90.7	4.2
EMI	130	190	1.46	120	63.2	(12.5)
Imp.Group	71½	89	1.24	100	112.3	1.5
RTZ	164	263	1.6	308	117.1	67.8
	Average		1.33		103.0	6.77

shares in the list. That is not bad by any standards, especially considering that we have operated purely on prices, without reading any news about the various companies' performances in terms of turnover, profits, takeover bids or any of the other information so dear to the hearts of the fundamentalists.

If we had bought the best performing option series in each of these six shares, we would have made an average gain of 110.6%, about *nine times* that in the actual shares themselves. More realistically, by taking an average of all the available series in the shares, the gain would have been 75.5%, about six times the gain in the share themselves.

The relationship between share prices and option prices is shown in Fig. 10.1, which plots the Marks & Spencer share price and the prices of the October

Table 10.4. Shares from the traded options list which have above average volatility and strength

.Share	% gain in share price, 9 Mar. – 11 May 1979	% gain in best option	Average % gain for all option series
BP	11.2	45.9	34.8
GEC	13.9	173.1	117.2
Grand Met.	15.7	123.1	74.1
Land Securities	7.3	82.6	52.6
Marks & Spencer	21.8	157.1	115.8
Rio Tinto Zinc	7.8	82.6	58.4
Average	12.95	110.7	75.5

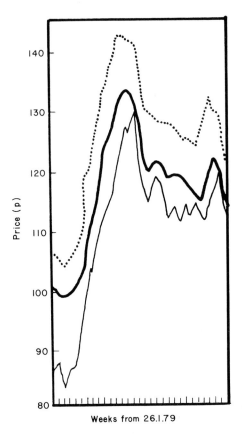

Figure 10.1. Traded options: light line, share price of Marks & Spencer; heavy line, the price of the October 90s option with 90p added; broken line, the price of the October 80s option with 90p added (90p is added instead of 80p in order to avoid overlap with the 90s option trace).

80 and October 90 series from 26th January, 1979 onwards. Since we are most interested in percentage gains, the percentage gain from the starting date of the graphs is shown on the right hand axis, with the prices at the left. We can see that the share price made approximately a 50% gain from this point by May 4th, the peak of the share price. The October 80s made a 330% gain and the October 90s about a 225% gain. The shapes of the curves for the two series are almost identical, and have almost a constant difference of about 9p. The option prices peak out at the same time that the share price peaks out, but an interesting point is that the share price retreated about 42% from its peak, but the option prices fell back 57% from their peaks. Thus in a rising share market, the option market seems to be over-optimistic, but becomes pessimistic in a falling share market.

So far, we have only discussed the gains which would have been made in these option series by using the 13-week moving average of the FT Index to generate a buying signal. This signal is of course the one which we have recommended for the 'cautious' investor to use. Now it is debatable whether the adjective 'cautious' can be applied to those who use the traded options market. It is probably more appropriate that investors in the traded options market be described as 'aggressive', so that they should use the 5-week moving average. As far as early 1979 is concerned, the 5-week moving average of the FT Index turned up a week earlier than the 13-week one, on 2nd March. Buying at this time would have resulted in much cheaper prices, both for the shares themselves, and for the various option series. The gains which would have resulted from investment on 2nd March 1979 in the six companies which we chose earlier on the grounds of volatility and strength are shown in Table 10.5, which should be compared directly with Table 10.4.

The extra week gained at the beginning of the rise in the market resulted in a gain of about 50% on the average gains for the share prices, best option prices and the average for all the option series. The same comment applies here though as for shares as far as the 5-week moving average is concerned. It will lead to greater profits on those occasions when it correctly foretells a prolonged upturn in the market, but often it can be wrong, thus introducing a greater element of risk. It is simply a matter of personal preference as to whether you are prepared to take a greater risk in order to give yourself the potential for a larger profit.

An interesting way to picture the market's thinking about the share price during its rise and fall is to add the striking price and the contract price. This value gives an idea of what the market thinks the share price will reach in the weeks ahead before the series expires. In this context the market means the balance point between those buying options, who think the market will rise, and those writing options, who think the market will fall. In Fig. 10.2 is plotted the actual share price for Marks & Spencer and the price of the October 90 series, with 90p added to the latter. Obviously, at the end of January, when the

Table 10.5. Shares from the traded options list which have above average volatility and strength

Share	% gain in share price 2 Mar. – 11 May 1979	% gain in best option	Average % gain for all series
BP	19.3	129.0	106.0
GEC	21.2	212.9	172.9
Grand Met.	21.3	153.3	117.0
Land Securities	9.2	86.4	61.8
Marks & Spencer	33.7	311.1	225.4
Rio Tinto Zinc	11.4	89.6	113.7
Average	19.4	163.7	132.8

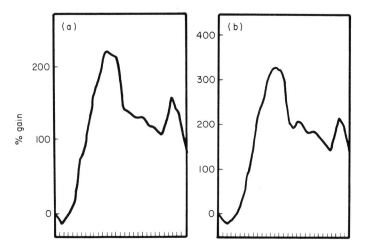

Figure 10.2. (a) The % gain in the Marks & Spencer October 80s option. (b) The % gain in the Marks & Spencer October 90s option. Gains are relative to the price at 26th January 1979.

share price was 85p, the market expected it to reach 100p between then and the expiry date. By mid-April, when the share price was in the high 120s, the traded options market saw it reaching only a fraction higher, to 133p between then and October. By the end of August, the market expectation was for a peak of 110p. At the beginning of the rise in February, therefore, the options market was highly optimistic, seeing a price rise of about 18% in Marks & Spencer shares, but by the end of April the expectation was for only another 6% gain. By the end of August when the share price was 108p, the market could see only a rise to 110p, a gain of less than 2%.

Since our whole attitude to the stock market is one of attempting to predict whether share prices are going to go up or down, we may well ask ourselves how good the traded option market is at this, since it is what the options market is all about. At the very least, the options market gives us a chance to test the thinking of a fairly large body of people — those who buy and sell options — against our own personal conclusions about the short-term future of shares. So, if the prices of options are rising, but we have concluded that the market is due for a fall, then this disparity needs to be checked out very carefully. This is not to say that we are necessarily wrong, since often it is the lone voice that is correct. It does mean that we have to be very sure of the facts upon which we have based our divergent opinion.

Since the traded options market has only been in existence for a year or so at the time of writing, there is not enough information available to determine how consistently successful the market is at predicting prices rather than simple rises of falls in the value of shares. If it is able to give us some idea of prices, then it adds a new exciting dimension to stock market investment. Hitherto, we have been able to draw conclusions about only two properties of share prices —

Table 10.6. Marks & Spencer share prices and prices predicted by the October 90 series traded options

Date	Share price	Traded options predicted price	Predicted peak as % of actual peak
26 Jan. 79	85	100	74.6
2 Feb. 79	87	99	73.9
9 Feb. 79	82	97 ½	72.8
16 Feb. 79	86	99	73.9
23 Feb. 79	86	99	73.9
3 Mar. 79	92	102	76.1
10 Mar. 79	103	109	81.3
17 Mar. 79	102	110	82.1
24 Mar. 79	109	117	87.3
31 Mar. 79	112	123	91.8
6 Apr. 79	114	125	93.3
13 Apr. 79	120	130	97.0
20 Apr. 79	127	132	98.5
27 Apr. 79	125	133	99.3
4 May 79	130	131	97.8
11 May 79	123	130	97.0

firstly that share prices have started to rise, and secondly that they have started to fall. Both of these occurrences tend to happen rather suddenly, so that we have virtually no warning that the market has taken off, but rely on moving averages confirming that the rise has started some weeks after the event. The same thing happens when the market tops out, it is not until passed the peak that the moving averages or the trend of the rise – fall indicator tell us what has happened. Another unsatisfactory point is that once we are certain that the market is headed upwards, we have only the haziest idea of how high the shares will rise, although we can get some information by the methods discussed in Chapter 11. Even when the trend upwards has been underway for some time, we have no information that would enable us to update our prediction as to the highest price that will be reached.

However, the traded options market does exactly that: the market is con- tinually updating its view of what the peak share price will be. Because of this aspect, we can now look at the options market in Marks & Spencer shares, as but one example, in a new light, namely how good is the market in predicting the peak price of Marks & Spencer? The difficulty is in deciding how to score such predictions. It is easy to say that if a price of 130p is predicted, and that is the exact peak that the market reaches, then the market is 100% right, but what prediction would make the market 100% wrong? Would it be a value of zero, a price which stays the same, or simply a fall in price instead of a rise? For our purposes we can adopt a system in which we express the predicted price as a percentage of the actual peak reached, which during the week ended 11th May 1979 was 134p. These data are given in Table 10.6; the figures are impressive,

Table 10.7. Share prices as predicted by the traded options market on 27 Apr. 79 and actual prices reached in the period to 31 Aug. 79

Share	Option	Predicted price @ 27 Apr. 79	Peak price reached up to 31 Aug. 79	Predicted price as % of actual
BP	Oct. 950	1304	1295	100.7
	Oct. 1000	1304		100.7
	Oct. 1050	1316		101.6
	Oct. 1100	1324		102.2
Commercial Union	Oct. 160	193	185	104.3
	Oct. 180	198		107.0
Consolidated Gold Fields	Oct. 180	259	268	96.6
	Oct. 200	259		96.6
	Oct. 220	265		98.9
GEC	Oct. 330	463	456	101.5
	Oct. 360	470		103.1
	Oct. 390	474		103.9
Grand Metropolitan	Oct. 100	183 ½	178 ½	102.8
	Oct. 110	183 ½		102.8
	Oct. 120	183 ½		102.8
	Oct. 130	183 ½		102.8
	Oct. 140	184		103.1
Land Securities	Oct. 240	330	323	102.6
	Oct. 260	331		102.4
	Oct. 280	333		103.1
	Oct. 300	343		106.2
Marks & Spencer	Oct. 80	132	134	98.5
	Oct. 90	133		99.2
	Oct. 100	136		101.5
Shell	Oct. 600	847	804	105.3
	Oct. 650	847		105.3
	Oct. 700	850		105.7
BOC	Aug. 60	83	81 ½	101.8
	Aug. 70	84 ½		103.7
	Aug. 80	88		107.9
Boots	Aug. 200	240	238	100.8
	Aug. 220	245		102.9
	Aug. 240	254		106.7
Imperial Group	Aug. 80	113	108	104.6
	Aug. 90	113		104.6
	Aug. 100	114		105.5
RTZ	Aug. 260	350	362	96.7
	Aug. 280	356		98.3
	Aug. 300	362		100.0

since they show that the options market, 2 weeks *before* the peak price was reached, was able to predict that price to within 99.3%, or 1p of the actual peak. Even 1 month before the peak, the traded options market was 93.3% correct, predicting a peak of 125p against the actual high of 134p.

Since the options market was most successful in the case of Marks & Spencer 2 weeks before the peak was reached, it is a worthwhile exercise to see how this market saw the prices of the other companies in the traded options list at that date, i.e. 27th April 1979. Remember the political background at that time was that we were 1 week before a General Election which the Conservative party were odds-on favourites to win. The vast majority of financial commentators saw the stock market continuing its strong upward movement in the event that a Conservative government was brought to power. Even if one or two commentators saw the upward trend diminishing, it is doubtful that many forecast that the top of the market for the time being would be reached the following week. So, the view of the options market that week imposed an extremely severe test of its ability to forecast peak prices.

The data for the various October and August series of the traded options are given in Table 10.7. For the various October and August series which were listed earlier in Table 10.2, Table 10.7 shows the share price as predicted by these options, and the actual peak price reached. Also shown is the predicted price as a percentage of the peak price. This value would be 100% for a correct prediction, and greater than 100% for those cases where the options market was over optimistic and predicted prices higher than those actually reached.

Three companies are missing from this list, namely Courtaulds, EMI and ICI, since the share price continued to fall after the date 27th April 1979 at which we have analysed the predictions. Hence there were no peak prices upon which to carry out any calculations. For the other 39 series shown in Table 10.7, the average predicted price was 102.4% of the actual peak price reached subsequently. In other words, the traded options market on 27th April predicted peak share prices for 12 companies that were within 2% of the peaks actually reached, and this at a time when most experts were entirely wrong about even the *direction* the stock market was going to travel, let alone how far it would go along the road! By any standards that was on exceptional achievement. Thus the traded options market gives us another tool in our quest for a better prediction of what the stock market is about to do. We should pay a great deal of attention to what this mini-market is saying, even if we do not intend to buy or sell options.

Chapter 11

Moving Averages as Predictors of Share Price Movements

So far in this book we have utilized moving averages as predictors of share price movements only in the simplest sense that when these averages turn up after falling for some time, then we can predict a general rise for some months ahead. Although we can never be absolutely certain that such a rise will occur, the odds are greatly in favour of such a rise because of the past behaviour of the market. In this chapter we are going to look more closely at individual share prices, with a view to deciding whether moving averages can be used to predict a price range into which a share price will move in the near future. Naturally, the odds against being able to predict a *price* for a share rather than just the *direction* of price movement must be considerably less in our favour. However, it should become clear that there is much to be gained from a closer study of moving averages.

We have already shown a chart of the 13-week moving averages of a number of shares, and one of these will serve again to illustrate a number of points. In the chart for Babcock & Wilcox shares shown in Fig. 11.1 are drawn 13-week and 103-week moving averages, as well as the weekly closing prices, for the period since 1970. Two important observations can be made about moving averages, and these can be clearly seen in Fig. 11.1.

1. The longer the averaging period, the smoother the resulting curve. Because of the mathematics of moving averages, the longer the period of time we use for averaging, the smoother will be the plot of the resulting averages. It would take several weeks or perhaps months of collapse of a share price before the 103-week moving average will start to turn down. Because of the way in which averages are calculated, the value for the average should be plotted half the span behind in time. Thus the 103-week average is plotted 1 year behind the present time. Although the peak price of 198p was reached in May 1979, it took another 30 or so weeks until the 103-week average topped out. On the other hand, the 13-week average, being much more

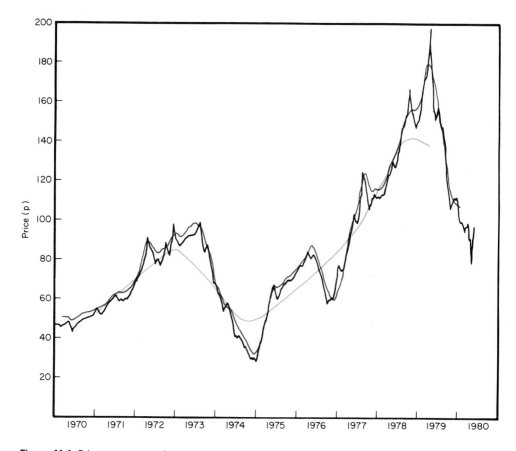

Figure 11.1. Price movements of the shares of Babcock & Wilcox since 1970. The 13-week moving average is shown in red and the 103-week moving average is in green.

responsive to a sustained fall in prices, was seen to turn down only a few weeks after the peak price was attained. The penalty for this extra smoothness attainable in a moving average plot is, of course, that the delay is so long before it reverses direction that it is entirely useless as a buying or selling signal. For example, by the time the 103-week average topped out, some 30 weeks after the peak price, the share price had fallen to around 110p, giving an unacceptable loss. On the other hand, the advantage of the smooth curve is that it is much easier to extrapolate by eye into the future, and it is this aspect which is so important in predicting future price ranges.

2. We can draw sensible limits for the extent to which prices move away from moving averages.

Figure 11.1 shows that the weekly closing prices of a share meanders about the 13-week average and the 103-week average, while the 13-week average also meanders around the 103-week average. We can draw reasonable limits for the extent to which prices move away from the 103-week average. The further away the price moves from this average, the greater is the probability that it will reverse direction and return to the moving average. This is easily demonstrated by looking at the differences between the share price and the 103-week moving average every week from the start of this average to its last point on the chart in Fig. 11.1. These are expressed as a percentage of the moving average value, ignoring the positive or negative nature of the difference, in the histogram shown in Fig. 11.2. This shows that for 54.1% of the time, the price was less than 10% away from the moving average, and for 79.0% of the time the price was less than 20% away from the moving average. This means that we can construct a band by drawing a line, following the 103-week average and 20% of its value higher, and a second such line 20% of its value lower. The price then stayed within this band 79% of the time. Of course, the figures will vary some-what from one share to another, since they will have different short-term volatilities. By combining these two features of ease of extrapolation and a limit where the chances are 80:20 that the price will not penetrate the limit, we can begin to formulate a method of using moving averages as an aid to prediction of prices.

In Fig. 11.3 the weekly closing prices for Babcock & Wilcox and the 103-week moving average are plotted. Superimposed on this are the two limit lines, above and below this moving average, representing price movements of ± 20% from the moving average. The main disadvantage in using this chart to test what decisions we might have made at various periods since 1970, utilizing the concepts we have developed, is that we have the benefit of hindsight. We can see that there were reversals of the 103-week moving average in early 1973,

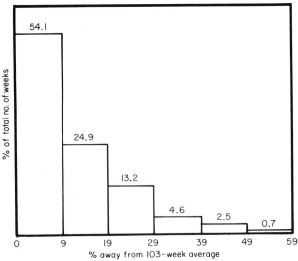

Figure 11.2. A histogram of the number of weeks the price of Babcock & Wilcox shares spent at certain percentages away from the 103-week moving average.

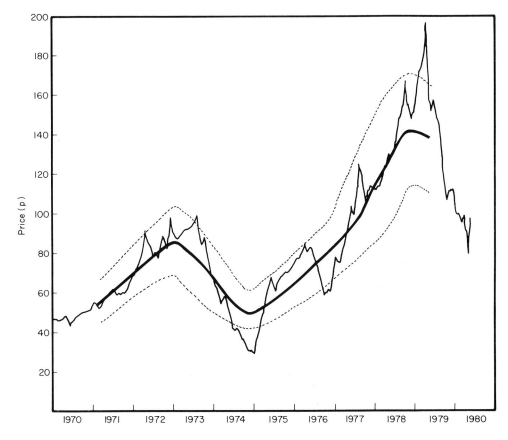

Figure 11.3. Babcock & Wilcox share prices for 1970 – 80. The 103-week average is shown as a solid heavy line. The dotted lines above and below the average represent the limits of 20% price movements away from the average.

early 1975 and late 1980. Of course, at those dates we would not have known that, since the averages would have been lagging behind by 1 year, for the reasons outlined earlier. A good exercise here to help with decision-making is to cover with a sheet of paper all that chart to the right of a specified time in which we are interested. At that particular time we also need to erase mentally the moving average and limit lines for a whole year backwards in time. If we suppose that we did that exercise for somewhere in the beginning of 1973, we would see the situation as drawn in Fig. 11.4. There is obviously, at that point, to tell us that the 103-week moving average will be turning down sharply in a year's time, although it is curving slightly, the slope decreasing constantly. Our efforts at extrapolation would produce the dotted lines shown in Fig. 11.4, and we could see that the price is near the predicted 103-week average, and not at either of the extremes. At such a point we are in neither a buy nor a sell situation, and in any case a glance at the chart as it would have been a couple of

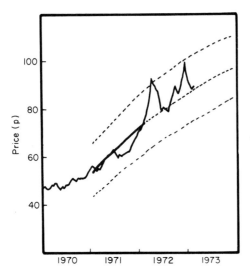

Figure 11.4. Babcock & Wilcox share prices for 1970–73. The 103-week average is shown, along with its projection into the future. The 20% price limit above and below the average are shown as dotted lines.

months earlier shows that we would have sold then. This is because we would have been out towards the upper limit which we would have been predicting to be about 100p. At such a point the chances are about 80:20 that the price will retreat towards the value of the average itself. Caution would dictate that we wait for the price to retreat slightly, in order to cover for the 20% chance that the price will rise even further.

To return to the present point, we are presented with two possibilities: either the price will rise again from its value near the average towards the upper limit which will be somewhere between 105 and 110p, or it will fall towards the lower limit which is around 80p. In fact the price rose to just below 100p, but then suffered a sustained fall for over a year.

Another point of interest on the chart in Fig. 11.3 is that at the end of 1974 and beginning of 1975. The situation as we would have been plotting it at the time appears in Fig. 11.5. Once again, we would not be able to predict the upturn that then transpired in the 103-week moving average, and this upturn would not have become obvious until a year later. We would almost certainly have extrapolated the moving average and the upper and lower limits as shown in Fig. 11.5. By doing this we would see that the actual share price is somewhere near the predicted lower limit of 30p. We would therefore have been starting to think of this as a buying opportunity, since the chances are much more in favour of a rise back towards the moving average than for a further fall. We would of course wait for a positive sign that such a rise was underway by watching for a slight rise back from the present position. By doing this we

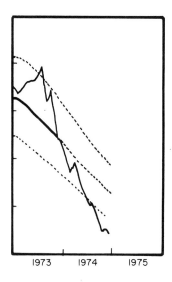

Figure 11.5. Babcock & Wilcox share prices for 1973 – 75. The 103-week average is shown, along with its projection into the future. The 20% limits above and below the average are shown as dotted lines.

would have bought in at around 35p, and would have sold in mid-1975 at around 68p for a very useful profit. You may ask why we would have sold at this point, since the chart in Fig. 11.3 shows the 103-week average rising strongly, with very much further to go. The reason is that at that time in mid-1975, we had no firm indication that the 103-week average had turned up from its downward trend. We might have expected a turn up, since the share price of 68p was so far out of line from a predicted price of about 40p that this must eventually work its way into the average, but on the other hand this high price may well have turned out to be a temporary peak. However, the first sign of a retreat from this high point would have been an indication to sell, since the odds were against a further upward trend in the short term.

Between 1975 and 1979 there were two more trading opportunities signalled by the moving average, in late 1976 and late 1977. A predicted 103-week moving average, and the upper and lower limits for this period are shown in Fig. 11.6. Towards the end of 1976, the price had fallen below the boundary of the extrapolated lower limit. A rise towards the average then signalled a good buying opportunity at about 65p. Depending on the slope of this upward trend, the price could be expected to move into a range somewhere between 100p and 120p. With a hiccup at 100p, which presumably forms some kind of psychological barrier (note earlier unsuccessful attempts to rise above this) the price reached the predicted upper limit in late 1977, and then retreated back towards the average. Thus a gain of nearly 100% could have been made by buying and

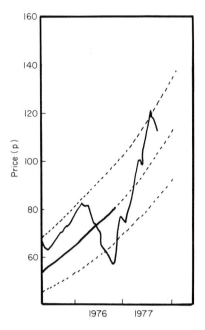 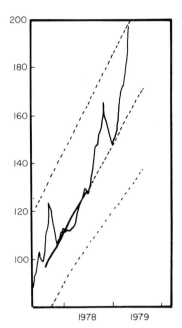

Figure 11.6. Babcock & Wilcox share prices for 1976 – 77. The 103-week average is shown, along with its projection into the future. The 20% limits above and below the average are shown as dotted lines.

Figure 11.7. Babcock & Wilcox share prices for 1978 – 79. The 103-week average is shown, along with its projection into the future. The 20% limits above and below the average are shown as dotted lines.

selling operations based on these predictions.

A significant feature of Fig. 11.3 is of course the peak price briefly attained in May 1979, which was followed by a rapid collapse in price. This is a critical test for the value of predictions based on moving averages, since a wrong decision at this point in time would have led to a catastrophic halving of the value of an investment in Babcock & Wilcox over the following year.

An inspection of Fig. 11.7, which shows how the position would have looked in May 1979, indicates that the price of 198p was about touching the upper limit which would be obtained by extrapolation of the 103-week average and its limits. Hence the chances of a further rise at that point are 80:20 against, and a slight retreat in price should have been taken as an indicator to sell. We would have been able to have come out from Babcock & Wilcox at somewhere around 190p, so that we can say without qualification that an analysis of the 103-week moving average and the limits within which the price spends about 80% of its time were successful in preserving the capital gain made by previous successful buying operations.

One final point at which we should make a prediction, and at which the reader will be able to check for accuracy, is the position at the time of writing, in May 1980. In the chart in Fig. 11.3 the moving average and higher and lower

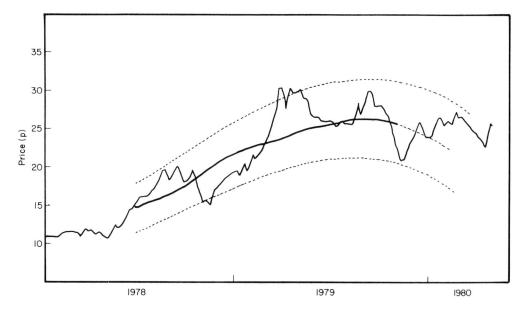

Figure 11.8. Share prices for Energy Services and Electronics for 1978 – 80. The 103-week average is shown, along with its projection into the future. The 20% limits above and below the average are shown as dotted lines.

limits have been extrapolated. It can be seen that the present price of 90p is very near to the extrapolated lower limit. A rise from this point towards the average would be a definite buying signal, and, if such a signal occurs during May and June, the price would be expected to rise into the range of 110–120p over the short term.

So far we have been utilizing an average which has a fairly long span — 103 weeks being of course the nearest odd number of weeks to 2 years. However, a shorter span, say 1 year, can also give useful results, since it should be, in most cases a reasonably smooth plot, capable of good extrapolation. An example of this is shown in Fig. 11.8, where the weekly closing prices of Energy Services and a 51-week moving average are plotted. A calculation shows that in this case for 85% of the time the weekly prices are within 20% of the moving average, as shown in Fig. 11.9. The upper and lower limits of this 20% movement are also plotted on the chart. We can say that when the price has reached one of these limits, there is an 85:15 chance that the price will tend to return back to the average. We can carry out a procedure similar to that employed in the last case, and cover up the chart to the right of the point of interest, bearing in mind that the last value we would have for the 51-week moving average would be 26 weeks (half a span) back in time. By doing this we would find a buying situation in November 1978 as the price rebounded from a slight penetration of the lower limit. The selling situation occurred in March 1979 as the price fell back through the upper limit. The next buying time was in November 1979 when

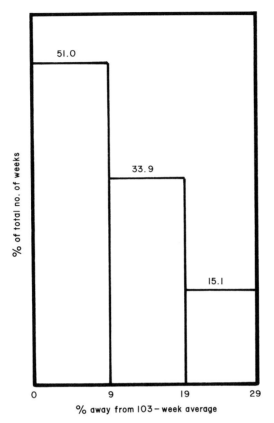

Figure 11.9. A histogram of the number of weeks the price of Energy Services and Electronics spent at certain percentages from the 103-week moving average.

the price rose from its brief contact with the lower limit at about 21p. The shares should have been sold in March 1980 when the price came near to the extrapolated upper limit of $27\frac{1}{2}$ p. Although the price fell from that point, it did not even penetrate the 51-week average, and so has not generated a buying signal up to the time of writing.

Although it is difficult to generalize, it is unlikely that a moving average with a span less than 1 year (51 weeks to the nearest odd number; an odd number is necessary otherwise the result would have to be plotted halfway through a week) will give good results. A choice between 51 weeks and any other larger value such as 103 weeks (2-year span) will depend upon the time interval between important highs and lows in the chart of the share price. For the mathematically minded we can describe in more detail how a decision can be made upon the span of the average. First of all we may ask why moving averages are of use at all in predicting price movements. The answer lies in the fact that they act as filters, although not as good as others which we can design to do the

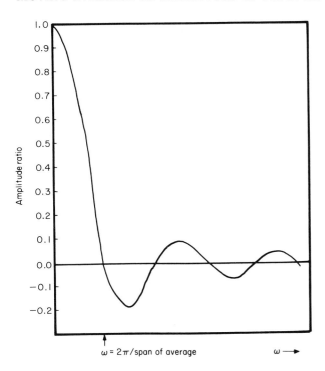

Figure 11.10. Frequency response of a moving average.

job. If we are reasonably happy that share prices have ups and downs which are not totally random, but exhibit a number of periodicities that may be complex, but capable of resolution, then such filters can be used to resolve these periodicities. Thus if we feel that a share price exhibits fluctuations that indicate fairly dominant components of, say, 31- and 51-week periodicity, then a 31-week moving average will filter out the component of 31-weeks periodicity and highlight the 51-week component. A 51-week moving average will remove the 51-week component and highlight components of even longer duration. Because these filters are not perfect, we will still see traces of higher frequencies coming through, although they may be out of phase. Thus with the 51-week average, there could still be a proportion of the 31-week component apparent in the average, although it will be attenuated compared with the original before applying the average.

An idea of the frequency response of a moving average can be gained from Fig. 11.10, where amplitude ratio is plotted against ω ($\omega = 2\pi/t$, where $t =$ time). Figure 11.10 shows that a cut-off point occurs where $\omega = 2\pi/$ (span of the average). (An amplitude ratio of 1.0 means that that frequency is passed with no attenuation, where an amplitude ratio of 0 means a complete cut-off for that frequency.) We can see from the figure that frequencies lower than the cut-off point will come through attenuated, with such attenuation getting less as the frequency gets lower. Thus, as an example, a 51-week average would cause components with, say, a 55-week periodicity to be almost cut-off, those with 103-week periodicity to be passed out considerably diminished, and those with say 401-weeks periodicity to be hardly affected. On the other hand, slightly higher frequencies, say of 41-week periodicity, would come through sharply attenuated and 180° out of phase, i.e. apparently inverted. At even higher frequencies the responses are even more diminished, but come back into phase again. At higher frequencies again the output moves out of phase, and at even higher frequencies back into phase. Of course the highest frequencies we would be interested in, since we are taking weekly closing prices, are for an ω value equivalent to 1 week, i.e. $\omega = 2\pi/1$, $\omega = 6.28$.

The only variable we have in deciding on a moving average is the length of the span of the filter. There are other more superior digital filters available which rely upon weighted values with which to multiply the share prices over the span of the filter. These entail a great deal of calculation, and are suitable only where a microcomputer is available, as discussed in the final chapter. Programs are available* commercially to carry out such operations, and the results obtained are really impressive, as can be demonstrated by the trace in Fig. 11.11. This is carried out on the same data for Babcock & Wilcox as was used for the 2-year moving average, shown in Fig. 11.1. The availability of a microcomputer (or larger mini- or mainframe computer) especially with disk storage will allow large amounts of data to be kept and research to be carried out on the cyclical movements of share prices.

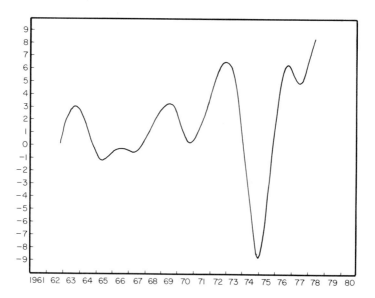

Figure 11.11. Application of a superior digital filter to the share prices of Babcock & Wilcox. The response is based on a 199 point weighted filter, covering the period from 1961 to 1980.

*From Lombardy Computers.

Appendix A

Chart Patterns

The charting of the price movements of a share over a long period of time can be of great value in aiding investment decisions, for both buying and selling operations as we have seen with moving averages. Chartists also maintain that certain patterns repeat themselves from time to time, not only in the charts of one particular share, but in those of other shares as well. Thus they argue that if one sees a pattern emerging, it is a reasonable bet that the trend will continue in the same way that it has done on previous occasions, and a decision can be based on this. There is something to be said for this view, as can be confirmed by studying charts of several shares, going back, say, 10 years. However, for our purposes, it is best not to follow patterns too slavishly, but to read them in conjunction with the other signals which we are receiving. If the chart patterns confirm the feeling we have from studying moving averages and 9-week lows etc., then we can proceed with even more confidence. If, however, the various signals are conflicting with each other, then, in the case of buying, it would perhaps be wiser to find some other share for which all the indications are positive. In a selling situation, it may pay to wait a little longer until the situation has clarified. What one must not do is base our decisions entirely on patterns.

In the following pages are described some of the most common patterns, and their implication for buying and selling. Of necessity a very simple view is given, and anyone wishing for more than this is advised to read carefully the many books available on technical analysis.

1. Support line (Fig. A.1(a))

This pattern is characterized by a price fall to a certain level, a reversal to a higher level, the process being repeated several times. The lower level is thus a support line, a point at which buyers appear who adjudge the share to be a good buy. If we can find such a pattern on the chart, then the time to buy would be just after the price has bounced up slightly from the point where we judged the line should be drawn. We should not consider buying before this in case the

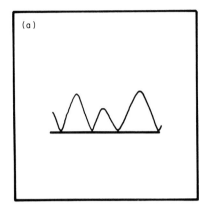 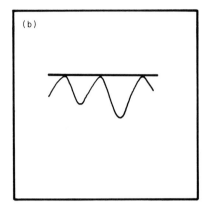

Figure A.1. (a) Support line; (b) resistance line.

support line is penetrated, i.e. it is not a support line any longer! This is discussed under heading 4. Note that we cannot expect a price to bounce up from a support line too many times. If it has already done so five or six times, say, then we should leave it alone. In common with other patterns discussed in this chapter, it is imperative to recognize them at an early stage in their formation, otherwise they can turn out to be traps for the unwary.

2. Resistance line (Fig. A.1(b))

We can regard this as the opposite of a support line. The price rises to a certain level, and then retreats before rising again back to that level. Several attempts may be made to penetrate the resistance line without success. The beginning of the fall back from this line is therefore a selling signal, indicating that the price has some way to fall. It is important to wait for a slight fall back from this line in case the line is penetrated (see heading 5).

3. Resistance becomes support (Fig. A.2)

Frequently, when a resistance line is penetrated upwards, the price eventually falls back to this line again before bouncing up again, and may repeat this action. The old resistance line has therefore become a support line. When a price penetrates a resistance line, its return back to this level should be watched carefully for the beginnings of a new upswing, since this would indicate a good buying level.

4. Penetration of a support line (Fig. A.3)

When a share price, having returned to a resistance level several times, finally penetrates it downwards, this is considered to be bad news, and the downward

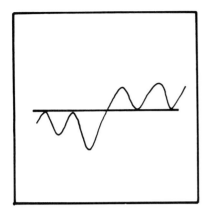

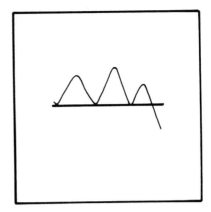

Figure A.2. Resistance line becomes support line.

Figure A.3. Penetration of a support line.

fall may be expected to continue some way. Such an action on the part of a share is therefore a selling situation.

5. Penetration of a resistance line (Fig. A.4)

When the price does not retreat on rising to a previous resistance line, but continues up through it, this is considered to be an important buying signal, and the shares, if already held, should not be sold.

6. Uptrend line (Fig. A.5)

This may be considered to be a support line which is sloping upwards instead of horizontal, with the price falling to this line and bouncing back up, repeating this performance several times. A slight bounce upwards from the line is therefore taken to be a buying signal, but no action should be taken until this happens since a downward penetration of the line is a selling signal, implying a further fall in the share price.

7. Downtrend line (Fig. A.6)

This is a downwards sloping version of the resistance line. The share price tends to rise to this line and then fall back. The beginning of the fall back is a selling signal, since the share price usually retreats considerably from this point. However, if the share price penetrates upwards through this line, this can be considered to be a buying signal.

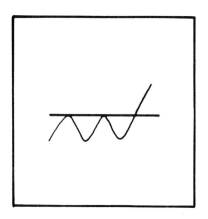

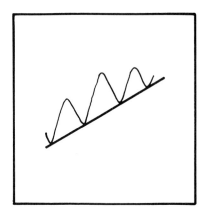

Figure A.4. Penetration of a resistance line.

Figure A.5. Uptrend line.

8. Curved uptrend line (Fig. A.7(a))

In this case the troughs of the upward waves, instead of falling on a straight line, fall onto a curve, the slope of which is beginning to flatten out. The same comments apply to this pattern as to straight uptrend lines, except that the flatter the curve becomes, the less is the possible rise from the line, and the more likely it is that the curve will turn over to become a downtrend line. The best course of action is not to use such a pattern as a buying indicator if the curve is obviously starting to flatten out, but if you have a holding in that particular share, watch closely until the curve turns downwards, and consider that to be a selling signal.

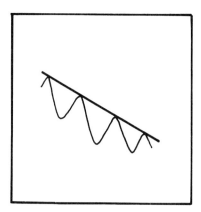

Figure A.6. Downtrend line.

9. Curved uptrend line (Fig. A.7(b))

The difference between this trendline and the previous one is that the curve line has only just started to curve upwards, and the amount of curvature is increasing. There is a greater chance that the line will continue to sweep upwards than in the case of 8, so a bounce up in the share price from this line constitutes a major buying signal.

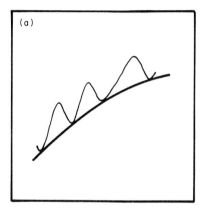 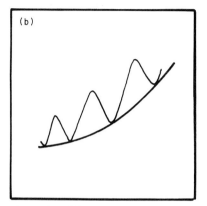

Figure A.7. Curved uptrend line: (a) curvature decreasing; (b) curvature increasing.

10. Curved downtrend lines (Fig. A.8(a) and (b))

These are curved varieties of the downtrend line 7. The peaks of the downward waves fall on a curved line instead of a straight line. As with 8 and 9, there are two versions of this, depending upon whether the curve downwards is increasing (a) or decreasing (b). If the latter, the downtrend may be coming to its end, so that a buying signal can be expected in the near future. If the curve is increasing, that is a major selling signal as soon as the share price retreats slightly from the line.

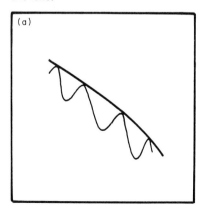 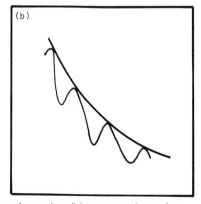

Figure A.8. Curved downtrend line: (a) curvature increasing; (b) curvature decreasing.

11. Uptrend channel (Fig. A.9)

This consists of two parallel lines, slanted upwards, between which the price yoyos. The lower line can therefore be considered to be a support line, while the upper line is a resistance line. A penetration of the lower line is a selling signal, since a further fall in price can be expected, while a penetration of the upper line is an indication of a further price rise.

12. Downtrend channel (Fig. A.10)

This consists of two parallel lines, slanted downwards, between which the price oscillates. The lower line is the support line, while the upper line is the resistance line. The same comments apply to this pattern as to the previous as far as penetration of the lines is concerned.

13. Head and shoulders (Fig. A.11)

This pattern consists of three waves, with the centre wave higher than the adjacent ones. We can draw a line through the two troughs — this is often called the 'neckline'. If the share price, after the right head wave, penetrates this neckline, this is taken to mean a further fall in price, hence such penetration is a major selling signal.

14. Double top (Fig. A.12)

The share price movement in this case is characterized by two peaks. During their formation, they might indeed to be the start of the head and shoulders pattern just discussed, but the fall in price below the previous trough, which does not happen with the head and shoulders, is a signal to sell.

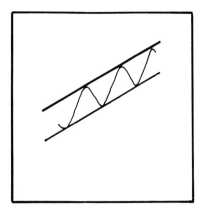

Figure A.9. Uptrend channel.

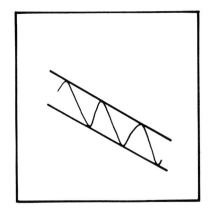

Figure A.10. Downtrend channel.

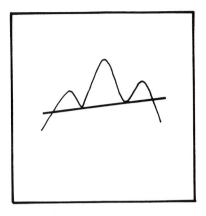

Figure A.11. Head and shoulders.

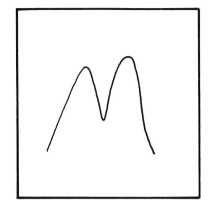

Figure A.12. Double top.

15. Spike top (Fig. A.13)

In this case the share price climbs rapidly to a peak, from which it falls just as rapidly. This is a dangerous formation, because of the usually rapid course of events. Just after the peak, it is not certain whether a double top or head and shoulders formation may be in the offing, but by the time realization sets in, a large loss could have been sustained.

16. Rounded top (Fig. A.14)

This is a much more comfortable pattern to be involved in than the previous type since the share price takes a long time to struggle over its peak. A late decision to sell in these circumstances can still result in only a limited loss of profit.

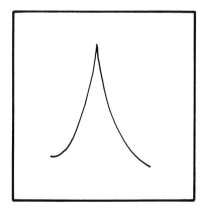

Figure A.13. Spike top.

Figure A.14. Rounded top.

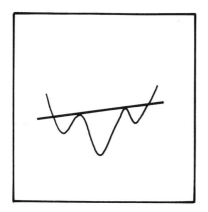

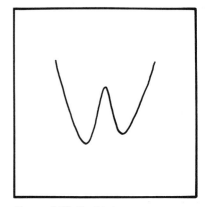

Figure A.15. Inverted head and shoulders.

Figure A.16. Double bottom.

The bottoming patterns are really just exactly the opposite of those just discussed and, of course, the opposite comments apply, in the sense that these represent buying opportunities rather than signals to sell. The inverted head and shoulders is shown in Fig. A.15, double bottom in Fig. A.16, 'V' bottom in Fig. A.17 and saucer bottom in Fig. A.18.

The charts of share prices over a long period of time usually show several of the patterns we have been discussing. We have used John Brown shares to illustrate many aspects of this book, hence it is appropriate to point out the occurrence of many chart patterns in the 10-year period since 1970, as shown in Fig. A.19.

In the first half of 1971 a *double bottom* pattern can clearly be seen. The first bottom was at 105p, and the second at 107p. The price subsequently rose to 182p so that the double bottom was an indication of a substantial price rise in a share which had been falling throughout the previous year. Throughout 1972 and 1973 the price fell several times to a *support level* of 130p and bounced up several times to a *resistance level* of about 175p. Once the support level was

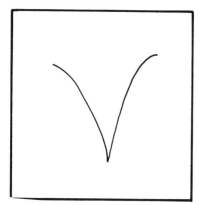

Figure A.17. 'V' bottom.

Figure A.18. Saucer bottom.

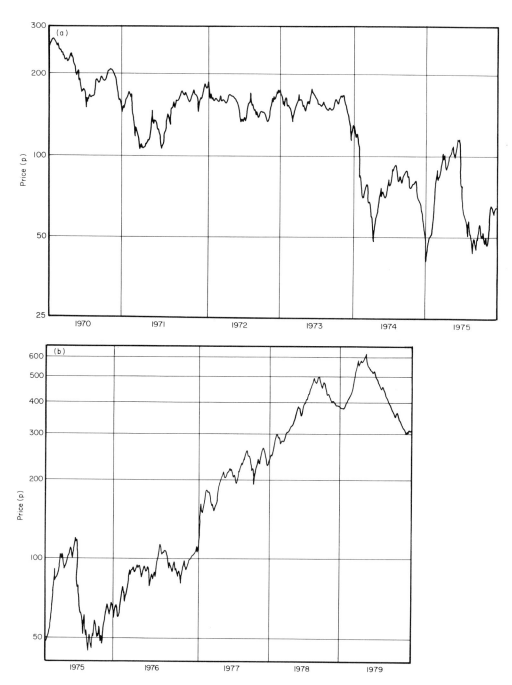

Figure A.19. Share price of John Brown (a) from 1970 to 1975, (b) from 1975 to 1979 (prices are on a logarithmic scale).

penetrated in late 1973 the price fell drastically to a low of 42p. A large *inverted head and shoulders* can be seen taking the two years 1974 and 1975 for its completion. A rise above the inverted neckline in 1976 saw the price rise up to nearly 600p in 1979. The price oscillations during 1977 and 1978 are part of a *curved uptrend* line.

In the chart of Babcock & Wilcox over the past 10 years (Fig. 11.3) a number of features can again be distinguished. A long *uptrend line* continued from mid 1970 until 1973. A *rounded top* formation is apparent during 1973 which eventually led to a closely spaced double bottom in late 1974. This was followed by a very substantial rise through 1975 and 1976. A good illustration of an *uptrend channel* can be seen during 1977.

These two examples serve to illustrate quite well the various types of pattern we have been discussing in this chapter. Of course we could present the chart of virtually any share price and find similar examples. We could also give examples to show that such patterns are not always indications of the future course of events, but it can be left to the reader to find those points in the John Brown and Babcock & Wilcox charts where a reliance on the pattern could have led to disaster. Remember we are working here with the benefit of hindsight; but to put yourself in the position as it would have been at the time, it would be instructive to cover the chart with a sheet of paper, and then slowly move it to the right so that the share price then unravels. Now test yourself by asking yourself frequently what investment decision you would take based upon what you can see up to that point. Hopefully this exercise will have a sobering effect upon any thoughts you might hold that charts of share prices offer a quick way to riches. We can but reiterate our statement at the beginning of this chapter — read patterns in conjunction with all the other signals and information available to you!

Appendix B

Microcomputers and the Smaller Investor

The sales of microcomputers in the UK over the last few years have risen dramatically, and can expect to rise at an ever increasing rate in the immediate future. There are two main reasons for this; firstly, the relatively low cost of these — from just under £100 for an 8K computer which can be plugged into the TV for displaying input and output, to about £3000 for a typical small business system with disk storage and printer — and, secondly, the saving in time and improvement in accuracy to be obtained in complex calculations and book-keeping, stock control, invoicing, payroll etc. The micro is ideal for repetitive calculations and for record-keeping and storage. It will have become apparent throughout the course of this book that these aspects have formed the very basis of our investment strategy. Besides this, the microcomputer can be used to keep track of the results of our investments, in the sense that it can record our purchases and sales, the dividends we have received, when dividends are due, and calculate our capital gains (losses?) for tax purposes at the end of each tax year. Commercial programs are available for these tasks (see address in Appendix E).

As with any other sphere of activity, a lot of jargon is associated with micro-computers, such as 'floppy disks', serial interfaces, modems, '32K' etc., and hence it it worthwhile cutting through this before proceeding further.

The 'memory' of a computer is expressed Kbytes, meaning thousands of bytes. An 8K computer therefore has a memory capacity of about 8000 bytes. In fact, because computers are based on binary numbers, such a computer would have $2^{13} = 8192$ bytes of memory, but this is always called '8K'. Although not strictly correct, we can define a byte as a character, such as 1, or A, or %, or +; this enables us to present a microcomputer as a device which can hold a large number of characters in its memory. A set of instructions will occupy some of the memory. This set of instructions is called a program. The rest of the memory is free to store the results of its calculations, or to store numbers of letters input from the keyboard, or to store data read in from a storage device such as a floppy disk or cassette tape. The results of carrying out the instructions can be displayed on a TV screen, or VDU (visual display unit), printed out by a printer, or stored on disk etc. for access at a later date.

The vast majority of microcomputers are programmed in a language called BASIC, which unfortunately is not quite standard between computers. A program written for a Pet would require slight modifications to run on an Apple and a different modification to run on a Tandy TRS80. However, these differences are relatively trivial, and the great advantage of BASIC is that it is easy to learn.

Since moving averages have been the prime consideration in this book, a BASIC program to run on an Apple computer and calculate moving averages of any time span up to 1000 weeks is given in Table A.1. Also shown is some of the printout for a 5-week moving average. Although the program is stored on a floppy disk and can be run by entering RUN and the name of the program, any data for weekly prices which is entered from the keyboard is lost once the computer is shut off or another program is run. The program in Table A.2 however does not suffer from this disadvantage. The weekly data is stored in the program, and the advantage is that any moving average can be calculated without the laborious tasks of re-entering the prices. The data list can also be scanned for errors before the program is finally saved on disk.

An even better way of carrying out this operation is to have the price data stored in a named file. The name of the file, which can be the same as the share name, is then requested by the program, which reads it and carries out the calculations. Each week a master program requests that week's closing prices of say 100 shares that you are following, and uses this to update each individual share file. A program to carry out all the tasks and calculations summarized in Chapter 8 is now available commercially (Appendix E). This program automatically tells the investor when to buy, what to buy and when to sell! The only operation is to enter the FT Index each week, the data for the 200 most volatile shares once at some point in the falling market, and from then on enter the weekly prices of the shares which it has told you to buy. Could anything be simpler?

Table A.1. Simple program to calculate moving averages

```
]LIST

5     P = 0
10    DIM A (1000)
20    INPUT "NUMBER OF POINTS OF MOVING AVERAGE";N
25    FOR I = 1 TO N
30    INPUT "ENTER X: ";X
45    P = P + X
50    A(I) = X
60    NEXT I
70    PRINT "X= ";X, "AVGE= ";P / N
80    INPUT "ENTER X: ";X
83    IF X = −1 THEN 200
```

Table A.1. *(cont'd)*

```
85      P = P + X − A(1)
90      PRINT "X = ";X, "AVGE = ";P / N
100     FOR J = 2 TO N
110     A(J − 1) = A(J)
130     NEXT J
140     A(N) = X
170     GOTO 80
200     END
```

]

```
RUN
NUMBER OF POINTS OF MOVING AVERAGE 5
ENTER X: 12
ENTER X: 13
ENTER X: 14
ENTER X: 15
ENTER X: 16
X = 16              AVGE = 14
ENTER X: 15
X = 15              AVGE = 14.6
ENTER X: 14
X = 14              AVGE = 14.8
ENTER X: 17
X = 17              AVGE = 15.4
ENTER X: 18
X = 18              AVGE = 16
ENTER X: 18
X = 18              AVGE = 16.4
ENTER X: 19
X = 19              AVGE = 17.2
ENTER X: − 1
```

]

Table A.2. Program for retaining weekly prices and printing a moving average of the weekly data

```
LIST

10      DIM A(1000)
20      DIM B(1000)
200     FOR I = 1 TO 1000
210     READ D
220     IF D = 0 THEN 210
225     IF D = 99999 THEN 1000
230     A(I) = D
240     NEXT I
```

Table A.2. *(cont'd)*

```
1000  INPUT "NO. OF POINTS OF AVERAGE <ODD NO.>";C
1005  PRINT "BABCOCK INTERNATIONAL ";C;" WEEK MOVING AVERAGE"
1006  PRINT : PRINT
1007  PRINT "WEEK NUMBER PRICE MOVING AVERAGE"
1010  D = 0
1020  X = 1
1030  Z = 0
1040  FOR N = X TO (C + X - 1)
1050  IF A(N) = 0 THEN 9999
1060  Z = Z + A(N)
1070  NEXT N
1080  LET D = D + 1
1090  B(D + (C - 1) / 2) = Z / C
1095  PRINT D,A (D), ( INT (B (D) * 10) ) / 10
1110  X = X + 1
1120  GOTO 1030
4910  REM  1970 DATA
4912  DATA  48,50,52,49,48,48,51,47,47,47,49,48,51,51,49,47,44,51
4914  DATA  51,50,46,42,45,49,43,48,48,49,49,50,51,51,51,51,50,49
4916  DATA  50,53,51,51,50,52,51,49,52,50,51,50,50,50,50,51,0,0
4920  REM  1971 DATA
4922  DATA  53,55,57,57,56,55,53,53,52,53,54,53,53,55,53,56,57,59
4924  DATA  58,61,64,61,60,60,58,57,59,63,63,62,61,61,60,62,62,62
4926  DATA  62,61,62,59,63,63,61,60,61,62,63,63,66,64,65,67,70,0
4930  REM  1972 DATA
4932  DATA  68,70,67,69,71,75,77,81,80,77,80,84,88,87,94,92,94,91
4934  DATA  90,88,87,81,80,79,80,78,82,78,83,82,89,84,81,79,78,84
4936  DATA  80,81,85,91,87,85,83,86,83,83,83,83,91,100,95,95,0,0,
4940  REM  1973 DATA
4942  DATA  93,94,91,86,88,90,88,88,83,85,85,88,91,96,96,96,98,94
4944  DATA  94,98,98,98,94,94,98,94,96,94,96,94,96,98,101,99,96,94
4946  DATA  93,86,88,90,91,88,91,91,88,83,80,70,67,59,66,70,0,0
4950  REM  1974 DATA
4952  DATA  69,66,67,61,61,62,61,61,60,55,55,50,37,51,56,60,58,56
4954  DATA  53,55,55,53,55,46,43,42,45,50,51,46,42,38,38,43,53,43
4956  DATA  38,37,34,34,35,35,37,34,32,30,26,26,27,29,30,29,0,0
4960  REM  1975 DATA
4962  DATA  25,25,28,28,30,34,36,38,40,40,40,37,39,50,54,63,60,60
4964  DATA  60,68,69,69,69,68,68,63,63,61,60,59,54,53,59,65,70,70
4966  DATA  70,77,68,68,67,66,69,70,71,70,69,66,70,69,70,69,0,0
4970  REM  1976 DATA
4972  DATA  73,74,74,76,79,80,77,72,77,75,76,77,80,80,80,88,85,89
4974  DATA  89,88,89,81,79,81,84,80,83,80,84,82,79,77,75,70,65,66
4976  DATA  71,67,69,62,62,58,53,55,60,60,60,57,55,60,59,61,61,0
4980  REM  1977 DATA
4982  DATA  76,79,75,78,80,76,77,77,74,77,77,80,81,79,85,85,88,90
4984  DATA  92,92,104,106,102,104,102,104,99,103,98,96,110,110,
      118,125,125,140
4986  DATA  130,120,120,120,120,120,120,106,108,107,105,116,114,
      114,114,116,0,0
4990  REM  1978 DATA
```

Table A.2. *(cont'd)*

```
4992   DATA   116,112,112,113,113,115,112,109,109,116,111,113,
       113,116,117,114,123,128
4994   DATA   132,131,130,130,130,133,127,129,127,132,132,137,
       140,146,141,142,138,137
4996   DATA   148,148,149,151,152,166,157,152,146,149,154,162,162,
       158,153,147,0,0
5000   REM   1979 DATA
5002   DATA   151,151,155,151,152,143,145,150,160,169,169,172,
       169,166,174,180,192,198
5004   DATA   184,175,181,181,177,155,151,161,166,164,166,158,
       149,150,154,146,147,140
5006   DATA   131,120,125,128,122,119,115,109,106,109,108,106,101,
       111,108,104,0,0
5010   REM   1980 DATA
5012   DATA   100,105,112,108,99,98,101,99,107,106,102,96,94,93,98,99,
       93,99
6000   DATA   99999
9999   END
```

]

Appendix C

Glossary of Stock Exchange Terms

Account: the period into which the Stock Exchange transactions are divided (usually 2 weeks, sometimes 3 weeks).

After-hours dealings: dealings between members' offices after 3.30 p.m. when the Stock Exchange officially closes.

Arbitrage: the taking advantage of the different prices in different markets by buying in one market and selling in the other.

Averaging: buying more securities on a fall or selling more on a rise, so as to level out the price of bull or bear transactions.

Bargain: a sale or a purchase between a jobber and a broker.

Bear: one who sells securities not owned by himself in the expectation that they can be bought again at a lower price before delivery is due.

Bid: when there are more buyers than sellers, a price may be quoted as 'bid'.

Blue chip: a company which may be regarded as a fairly safe investment, usually one which is quite large and well established.

Broken amount: an odd amount, which is not a usual market quantity. A seller may have to accept less than the market price, as the costs of transfer are proportionately more than for even amounts.

Bull: one who buys securities in the expectation that they will rise in price. If his optimism is on the wane, and he is ready to take a loss, he is known as a 'stale bull'.

Call option: the right to buy shares after the purchase of a call option.

Calls: the amounts which may be still payable after allotment in order that the securities may be fully paid. Over a period of a few months there may be one or two, or more calls. Forfeiture of the stock may result in the failure to meet them.

Cash settlement: payment is due on the following day, unlike normal Stock Exchange Account transactions for settlement. Gilt-edged securities are normally paid for in this way.

Close price: a narrow margin between the bid price and the offered price.

Closing prices: the prices at the official close of the House, at 3.30 p.m. and business transacted after this close is at 'after-hours' prices.

Contango: a rate of interest paid for carrying over a transaction from one account to another.

Coupon: the warrant, which usually has pages of coupons attached, which must be presented before collection of interest or dividends on bearer securities. The 'Talon', the last item on the old sheet, must be presented before obtaining new pages of coupons.

Cum: means 'with'. If a price is quoted 'cum' it includes any recently declared dividend, a scrip issue, rights or any other distribution.

Difference: the balance due to or by a client when buying or selling a security during a stock exchange account.

Discount: the amount, below its par or paid-up value, by which a security is quoted, i.e. a 50p share, paid-up to 25p, is quoted at 22 ½p, standing at a discount of 2 ½p.

Dollar stocks: American and Canadian stocks and shares.

Dollar premium: the premium beyond the usual exchange rate paid for 'investment dollars', which have to be bought in order to pay for American, Canadian and other hard currency stocks.

Equity: ordinary shares, which normally take most of the profits and all the risks. The equity-holders retain what is left after the demands of any other classes of capital have been met.

Ex: means 'without'. A price quoted 'ex', excludes dividends recently declared, scrip issue, rights or any other distribution.

Free: without stamp and fee, which means that these expenses are paid by the seller, usually on the sale of small lot of securities. It also applies when transacting new securities in allotment letter form, free of stamp duty until they have to be registered.

Funds: British Government stocks (also known as 'gilt-edged').

Gilt-edged: British Government and other fixed-interest securities.

Instalment: new issues of securities are often paid for over a period of time, in application and allotment money, followed by one or more instalments.

Interim dividend: dividend payments may be spread over the year by distribution of an interim, or more than one interim, followed by final payment at the end of the year.

Jobber's turn: the difference between the buying and selling prices at which a jobber is ready to deal. If the price is 85 – 87p the turn is 2p. When calculating the cost of buying and selling this should be taken into account.

Kaffirs: South African mining and related shares.

Limit: a broker can be 'limited' by his client to buying at a stated maximum price or selling at a stated minimum price.

Limited market: when it is difficult to buy or sell, because of shortage of stock for example, one or more securities are described as a limited market.

Lists closed: application lists for public issues and offers for sale are for a certain time. Lists are closed when the time expires or the offer is fully subscribed.

Long: anyone who holds an amount of a certain stock.

Longs: government and similar stocks with repayment dates more than 15 years in the future.

Making a price: when a price is quoted or 'made' by a jobber, he is about to buy at the lower price and sell at the higher price, in a reasonable quantity.

Marketable amount: the number of shares or stocks which would be reasonable for a jobber to deal with, when he has quoted a price.

Marking: details or the price at which brokers and jobbers transact a bargain, is entered on a marking slip, which is used for recording business done in the Official List.

Mediums: government and similar stocks with repayment dates varying between 5 and 15 years.

Moneystocks: very short-dated gilt-edged or any other securities which fall due for repayment at a certain date in the very near future.

Name ticket: the form which states the registration details on the purchase of securities, which the broker who is buying must give to the seller.

New time: purchases or sales in one account for settlement in the next. This type of deal can be done during the last 2 days of the old account.

Nominal: when a jobber quotes a price, but is not prepared to deal, the price is known as nominal and is simply an *indication* of the price.

NTP: this stands for 'not to press' and means that the buyer has an agreement with the jobber not to press for delivery if this delayed beyond the usual time.

Offered: there are usually more sellers than buyers when a price is so much 'offered'.

One way: 'one way only' means that a jobber cannot deal both ways, but can only bid for or offer stock.

Opening prices: the prices quoted by the Stock Exchange every day, at the official opening for business.

Pitch: the place where one would find a jobber on the floor of the House.

Position: a jobber has a position when he is a 'bull' (holding stock) or is a 'bear' (short of stock).

Premium: a security is at a premium when the price is greater than its paid-up or par value.

Put and call option: the right to buy or sell shares under an option.

Put option: the right to sell shares after the purchase of a put option.

Renunciation: shareholders are usually given the opportunity of selling their rights, given to them by a company, if they do not want to take up the offer. Their rights are then 'renounced' to a buyer.

Scrip issue: a capitalization of reserves and retained profits in the form of a 'free' issue of shares.

Settlement: payment for securities is either for cash, on the day after purchase or sale, or account usually days after the end of the 2- or 3-weekly account.

Short: when stock which is not owned has been sold, one is known to be short.

Shorts: gilt-edged stocks due for repayment with 5 years.

Shunter: a broker who deals between London and other United Kingdom stock exchanges with securities which are quoted in both.

Small: when the price made to a broker by a jobber is for less than a usual market quantity of stocks or shares.

Stag: one who applies for new issues and sells his allotment at the beginning of dealings, at a profit or loss.

To open: an announcement that the order is to buy or sell, or to get someone else to 'open'.

Touch: the nearest price quoted between the jobbers, or the highest price bid by one, and the lowest offered by another.

Undated: Government and other stocks which have no fixed dates for their repayment. Sometimes known as 'irredeemables'.

Unquoted: Securities which do not appear in the Official List or monthly supplement. Transactions in these can be carried out under Rule 163 (1)(e).

Wide price: a greater than usual difference between bid and offered prices.

Appendix D

The Top 100 UK Listed Companies

	Company	Turnover 1978 (£m)	Pre-tax profit 1978 (£m)
1	BP	*11997	2186
2	Shell Transpt	11394	1712
3	BAT Indust.	6676	433
4	Imperial Chem.	* 4663	505
5	Unilever Ltd	3958	349
6	Imperial Gp	3433	131
7	BL Ltd	* 2602	3.19
8	Gen. Electric.	2343	325
9	Grand Metrop.	1850	116
10	Rio Tinto-Zinc	* 1823	272
11	Rothmans Int.	1800	80.6
12	Bowater Corp.	1720	87.0
13	Assoc.Brit.Fds	1678	77.6
14	Inchcape	1661	62.3
15	Guest Keen	1639	94.0
16	Reed Intl	1623	81.0
17	Courtaulds	1576	53.7
18	Dunlop Hldgs	1361	54.0
19	S & W Berisford	1342	31.4
20	Marks & Spencer	1254	118
21	Ranks Hovis	1228	32.1
22	BOC Intl	1196	66.5
23	Lonrho Ltd	* 1171	76.8
24	Grt Univ. Sts	1154	128
25	Tate & Lyle	1147	24.6

	Company	Turnover 1978 (£m)	Pre-tax profit 1978 (£m)
26	Allied Brew.	★ 1106	77.2
27	Thorn Elec.	1092	110
28	CT Bowring	★ 1088	33.0
29	Amal. Metal	★ 1058	6.12
30	BICC Ltd.	★ 998	47.1
31	Burmah Oil	★ 987	3.61
32	Sears Hlgs	981	65.5
33	P&O Steam	980	34.2
34	Unigate Ltd	974	31.5
35	Lucas Ind.	971	73.1
36	Tesco Stores	953	28.6
37	Tozer Kemsley	★ 916	5.76
38	Hawker Sidd.	★ 912	104
39	Bass Charrng.	★ 905	86.1
40	Boots Co.	884	107
41	Cadbury Shw.	★ 884	48.2
42	Distillers Co.	876	160
43	Beecham Gp	866	143
44	EMI Limited	★ 851	64.7
45	Trafalgar Hse	825	60.6
46	Thos Tilling	811	53.9
47	Metal Box	807	55.9
48	J Sainsbury	797	27.6
49	Tube Invests	★ 792	54.8
50	Dalgety Ltd	787	24.4
51	Brooke Bond	756	44.7
52	Wimpey Cons	★ 752	52.4
53	Spillers Ltd	728	8.49
54	FW Woolwth	724	46.5
55	Gill & Duffus	★ 713	20.4
56	Tarmac Ltd	★ 664	24.2
57	Babcock & W.	★ 657	32.3
58	A. Guinness	643	44.9
59	Coats Patons	★ 640	82.1
60	Brit.Elec.Trac.	631	67.1
61	Unit. Biscuits	★ 630	38.1
62	Plessey Co.	611	42.9
63	Hanson Trust	605	26.1
64	Harr. & Cros.	★ 579	23.3
65	Whitbread	573	43.5
66	Reckitt & C.	★ 557	56.9
67	Ready Mixed	★ 547	28.3

Company		Turnover 1978 (£m)	Pre-tax profit 1978 (£m)
68	Glaxo Hldgs	544	86.4
69	Assoc. Dairies	536	25.4
70	Trust Hse F.	★ 531	38.0
71	Booker Mc.	★ 523	25.0
72	Thos Borthwk	512	6.22
73	ICL Limited	509	37.5
74	Fitch Lovell	501	7.61
75	Hs of Fraser	493	34.7
76	Rank Org.	485	122
77	Ultramar Co.	★ 473	24.7
78	Pilkington Bros	470	71.7
79	Rowntree	★ 469	41.5
80	Delta Metal	★ 469	26.7
81	IMI Ltd	★ 467	34.4
82	Ocean Transp.	★ 459	39.1
83	Guinness Peat	445	11.1
84	Debenhams	443	16.5
85	Richard Cost.	★ 432	36.2
86	Johnson Matt.	427	18.9
87	F.M.C. Ltd	423	0.98
88	John Laing	★ 421	21.1
89	Jn Laing Ltd	★ 419	16.0
90	Turner & N.	★ 414	45.4
91	Vickers Ltd	★ 409	25.1
92	Wood Hall Tst	402	4.87
93	W.H. Smith	394	20.8
94	Taylor Wdrow	★ 392	22.4
95	Scot. & New.	390	35.0
96	Ladbroke Gp	★ 388	24.3
97	Nthn Eng.Ind.	★ 387	25.2
98	Dickinson Rob.	★ 383	21.9
99	Stenhouse Hlgs	371	10.6
100	Davy Corp.	371	25.4

★1977 (1976) figures.

Appendix E

Useful Information

Addresses
1. For lists of brokers:
   The Secretary
   The Stock Exchange
   London EC2
2. For charts of share prices:
   Investment Research
   28 Panton Street
   Cambridge CB2 1DH
   Tel: 0223 56251-3
3. For microcomputers and programs:
   Lombardy Computers Ltd
   121 High Street
   Berkhamsted
   HP4 2DJ
   Tel: 04427 4247

Reference books
1. *The Investor's Manual*
   Kay and Ward Ltd.
   21 New Street
   London EC2M 4NT
2. *The Hambro Company Guide*
   Investment Evaluator (UK) Ltd
   6 Broad Street Place
   London EC2M 7JH

Newspapers and periodicals
1. *Financial Times*, published Monday – Saturday
   (Monday's issue gives month for dividends of quoted shares)
2. *Investor's Chronicle*, published fortnightly

3. For a quick catch-up on the week's events:
   Sunday Times, business news section
   Observer, business news section
   Sunday Telegraph, business news section
4. Most daily newspapers carry at least a half page of business comment and share prices